Integrated Brand Marketing and Measuring Returns

Also by Philip J. Kitchen

Kitchen, P.J. (1997, reprinted 1999, 2000, 2002, 2003, 2005, 2007, 2008) *Public Relations: Principles and Practice*, International Thomson Business Press. ISBN 1-86152-091-3. Translated into Russian, May 2002.

Kitchen, P.J. (1999, reprinted 2001, 2004, 2005, 2007) *Marketing Communications: Principles and Practice*, Thomson Learning; ISBN: 1-86152-196-0.

Schultz, D.E. and Kitchen, P.J. (2000) *Communicating Globally: An Integrated Marketing Approach*, NTC Business Books, Chicago and Macmillan Business, Basingstoke. Hardback ISBN: 0-333-92137-2. Paperback ISBN: 0-333-92138-0.

—— Published as an E-book, Spring 2003. http://ebooks.ebookmall.com/title/communicating-globally-kitchen-schultz-ebooks.htm

Kitchen, P.J. and Schultz, D.E. (2001) *Raising the Corporate Umbrella*, Palgrave Macmillan, Basingstoke. ISBN: 0-333-92639-0.

Kitchen, P.J. and Proctor, R.A. (Editors) (2001) *Marketing: The Informed Student Guide*, Thomson Learning. ISBN: 1-86152-546-X.

Kitchen, P.J. Editor (2003) *The Future of Marketing: Critical 21st Century Perspectives*, Palgrave Macmillan, Basingstoke. ISBN: 0-333-99286-5.

—— Ibid., in Mandarin, 2004, ISBN 7-80207-036-8; paperback.

Kitchen, P.J. (Editor) (2003) *The Rhetoric and Reality of Marketing: An International Managerial Approach*, Palgrave Macmillan, Basingstoke. Hardback. ISBN: 0-333-98732-2.

Kitchen, P.J. (Editor) (2004) *Marketing Mind Prints*, Palgrave Macmillan, Basingstoke. ISBN: 1-4039-0682-3.

Kitchen, P.J. and de Pelsmacker, P. (2004) *Integrated Marketing Communications: A Primer*, Routledge, London. ISBN 0-415-31420-8 (hbk); 0-0415-31421-6 (pbk).

Schultz, D.E. and Kitchen, P.J. (2004) *Communicating Globally: An Integrated Marketing Approach*, NTC Business Books, Chicago. In Russian ISBN: 5-16-001938-3 (hbk); 0-8442-2522-3 (pbk).

Kitchen, P.J., de Pelsmacker, P., Eagle, L., Schultz, D.E. (2005) *A Reader in Marketing Communications*, Routledge, London. December 2005. ISBN: 0-415-35648-2 (hbk); 0-415-35649-0 (pbk).

Kitchen, P.J. (Editor) (2008) *Marketing Metaphors and Metamorphosis*, Palgrave Macmillan, Basingstoke. ISBN: 978-1-4039-9861-3.

Integrated Brand Marketing and Measuring Returns

Edited by

Philip J. Kitchen

First published 2010 by
PALGRAVE MACMILLAN

Palgrave Macmillan in the UK is an imprint of Macmillan Publishers Limited,
registered in England, company number 785998, of Houndmills, Basingstoke,
Hampshire RG21 6XS.

Palgrave Macmillan in the US is a division of St Martin's Press LLC,
175 Fifth Avenue, New York, NY 10010.

Palgrave Macmillan is the global academic imprint of the above companies
and has companies and representatives throughout the world.

Palgrave® and Macmillan® are registered trademarks in the United States,
the United Kingdom, Europe and other countries.

ISBN-13: 978-0-230-57734-3 hardback

This book is printed on paper suitable for recycling and made from fully
managed and sustained forest sources. Logging, pulping and manufacturing
processes are expected to conform to the environmental regulations of the
country of origin.

A catalogue record for this book is available from the British Library.

A catalog record for this book is available from the Library of Congress.

10   9   8   7   6   5   4   3   2   1
19 18 17 16 15 14 13 12 11 10

Printed and bound in Great Britain by
CPI Antony Rowe, Chippenham and Eastbourne

To many fine teachers at various times in my life who have inspired me with their encouragement and counsel.

Thank you.

Contents

List of Figures

List of Tables

Acknowledgements

My grateful thanks to the contributors for sharing their knowledge, expertise, wisdom, and understanding of integrated brand marketing, integrated communications, and measuring and evaluating these topics in relation to return on investment. This bringing together of leading practitioners and academics in this domain is absolutely essential to all businesses involved with marketing, branding, and communicating in today's fiercely competitive world. Undoubtedly, marketing is transitioning to new and ever more dynamic forms and is doing so in an environment characterised by ongoing globalisation.

I am indebted to the contributors who have provided, discussed, and clarified many areas associated with integrated brand marketing and measuring returns and critically engaged with how these are applied in today's world.

I acknowledge, with the contributors, the many individuals, companies, magazines, and journals who have assisted us by allowing material to be cited and shared. And I thank practitioners and colleagues who, through various means, have influenced development of the ideas herein expressed.

To all of you, thank you for your help, guidance, support, and encouragement in the expression and critique of ideas and practices in this book, and their relevance to practitioners and theorists of marketing, branding and communication in the twenty-first century.

Philip J. Kitchen

The editor, contributors, and publisher are grateful for permission to use or cite copyright material. Every effort has been made to trace all the copyright holders, but if any have been inadvertently overlooked, the publishers will be pleased to make the necessary arrangements and adjustments at the first opportunity.

Notes on the Contributors

Mark Balnaves
He is Professor and Senior Research Fellow in New Media at Curtin University of Technology in Perth, Western Australia. He conducted Australia's first adoption and diffusion study of the Internet, leading in to the establishment of Telstra's BigPond service and the Australian Capital Territory's TransACT broadband service. His expertise is in audience research and media theory. He is currently finishing a history of broadcast ratings with Tom O'Regan, University of Queensland, funded by an Australian Research Council Discovery grant, The Emergence, Development and Transformation of Media Ratings Conventions and Methodologies in Australia, 1930–2008. His publications include *Mobilising the Audience* (University of Queensland Press), *The Global Media Atlas* (BFI/Penguin, and translated into French and German), and *Media Theories and Approaches: A Global Perspective* (Palgrave Macmillan).

Peter M. Cain
This material was written while the author worked as Global Vice President of Econometrics at Millward Brown Optimor, where he was responsible for econometric analysis as well as product innovation and development. Prior to Millward Brown, Peter worked for ACNielsen as an International Modeling and Analytics Consultant. Before ACNielsen, he worked for IRI as a Senior Development Consultant. Peter began his corporate career at The Boots Company, the leading pharmacy retail chain in the United Kingdom, with a focus on sales models and forecasts.

Peter currently works as Vice President of Analytics for Market Share Partners (MSP) based out of the company's London operations, where he leads the European analytics team and spearheads MSP's global Consumer Packaged Goods (CPG) practice.

Peter received his BS and MS degrees in Economics from the University of Warwick and his PhD in Monetary Economics and Applied Econometrics from the University of Nottingham.

Philip J. Kitchen
Holds the Chair and is Professor of Strategic Marketing at the University of Hull Business School, and Director of the Research Centre for Marketing, Communications and International Strategy (CMCIS). In 2009 he was also Affiliated Professor of Marketing, ESC Rennes, France; and Visiting Professor of Marketing at the University of Salerno, Italy, and University of Athens, Business, Greece. He is the Founder and Editor of the *Journal of Marketing Communications*, first published in 1995. He has published 11 books and over 100 academic papers in leading journals around the world. In 2003 he was listed as 'one of the top gurus who have influenced the future of marketing' (*Marketing Business*). In 2008, he tied for sixteenth place in the world in terms of comparative author ranking in the domain of advertising, *Journal of Advertising*, 37 (3), p. 85.

Professor Kitchen is a Fellow of CIM, the RSA, the Higher Education Academy, and Member of the Marketing Science Institute, and of the Institute of Directors.

This book is one of a series published by Palgrave-Macmillan. Previous books in the series were:

- *The Future of Marketing* (2003)
- *The Rhetoric and Reality of Marketing* (2003)
- *Marketing Metaphors and Metamorphosis* (2004)
- *Marketing Mind Prints* (2008)

Kitchen serves on many editorial review boards including *Journal of Advertising, Journal of Marketing Management,* and *European Journal of Marketing*. His research interests lie in marketing theory, integrated marketing communications, branding, and global marketing.

Don E. Schultz
Don E. Schultz is presently Professor Emeritus-in-Service of Integrated Marketing Communications at the Medill School of Journalism, Northwestern University. He is also President of the consulting firm, Agora, Inc. both located in Evanston, Illinois. Schultz maintains a busy academic life. In addition to his duties at Northwestern University, he hold visiting professor appointments at Queensland University of Technology in Brisbane, Australia; Cranfield University in Milton Keynes, England; Tsinghua University in Beijing, China;

and is a frequent guest lecturer at the Swedish School of Economics, Helsinki, Finland.

Following his graduation from the University of Oklahoma with a degree in Marketing/Journalism, Schultz began his career as a sales promotion writer for trade magazine publishers in Dallas. From there, he moved into publication sales and management, and was advertising director of a daily newspaper in Texas. He then joined Tracy-Locke Advertising and Public Relations in Dallas in 1965. He was with the agency for almost 10 years in its Dallas, New York, and Columbus, Ohio offices as branch manager. He served as management supervisor for a number of national consumer product, service, and industrial accounts.

In 1974, Schultz resigned as Senior Vice President of Tracy-Locke to launch a career in academia. He obtained a Master's Degree in Advertising and a Ph.D. in Mass Media from Michigan State University while also teaching in the MSU Department of Advertising. He joined Northwestern in 1977.

Schultz has consulted, lectured, and held seminars on integrated marketing communication, marketing, advertising, sales promotion, brands and branding, and communication management in Europe, South America, Asia, the Middle East, Australia, and North America. His articles have appeared in numerous professional trade publications and academic journals including *Advertising Age*, *Journal of Advertising Research*, *Journal of Advertising*, and *Marketing News*. Professor Schultz was the founding editor of the *Journal of Direct Marketing*. He is an Associate Editor of the *Journal of Marketing Communications*, and on the editorial review board for a number of trade and scholarly publications. He is also a regular columnist for *Marketing News* and *Marketing Management*.

He is author/co-author of 13 books, *Strategic Advertising Campaigns* (now in fifth edition), *Essentials of Advertising Strategy* (now in third edition), *Essentials of Sales Promotion* (now in third edition), *Sales Promotion Management*, *Strategic Newspaper Marketing*, and *Measuring Brand Communication ROI*. His book, *Integrated Marketing Communications* was the first text in this emerging field.

Schultz is former director of the Promotion Marketing Association of America and past Chairman, Accrediting Committee, Accrediting Council in Journalism and Mass Communications. He has also served as Director, Institute of Advanced Advertising Studies, as public member on The National Advertising Review Board and was a founding member of the Board of Directors of the Virginia Commonwealth University's Ad Center. He is also co-chair of the IMC Committee of the Advertising Research Foundation. He was selected the first Direct Marketing Educator of the Year by the Direct Marketing Educational Foundation. He was named Educator of the Year by the Chicago Chapter, Sales and Marketing Executives Association. American Advertising Federation named him Distinguished Advertising Educator of the Year. *Sales and Marketing Management* magazine named Schultz one of the '80 Most Influential People in Sales and Marketing'. He is also a member of the American Marketing Association, American Academy of Advertising, Advertising Research Foundation, Association for Consumer Research, Business Marketing Association, Direct Marketing Association, and the International Advertising Association. He is past Chairman, Communications Committee, Illinois Division, and the American Cancer Society.

Schultz has served on the board of directors of a number of corporations, including Penton Media, Inc., Cleveland; The Simon Richards Group, Melbourne, Australia; Brand Finance plc, London; Insignia Systems, Inc., Minneapolis; and dunnhumby associates, London.

Schultz resides in Evanston with his wife and business partner, Heidi.

Joanna Seddon is Founder and CEO of Millward Brown's global brand consulting practice, MB Optimor, that addresses clients' brand and business strategy and investment issues. She has more than 20 years of experience in providing strategic recommendations with measurable financial impact to leading clients worldwide.

In her role at Millward Brown, Joanna has been responsible for development of fresh approaches to maximizing the financial value of brands and marketing. She has also created the BrandZ Top 100 ranking of the world's most valuable brands, published annually in the *Financial Times*.

Prior to joining Millward Brown, Joanna was a founding partner and Executive Vice President for Worldwide Brand Strategy at FutureBrand. Joanna also led a cross agency group within IPG dedicated to creating best practices in marketing accountability.

Joanna has worked with the world's leading brands across a wide range of categories – from Procter & Gamble and Unilever to Coca Cola, Bacardi, Visa, Bank of America, Vodafone, UPS, and AT&T.

Joanna made the move from strategy consulting in the UK to the US, to lead the successful turnaround and sale of a division of McKesson Corporation, a global leader in supply chain management.

Joanna holds a D.Phil. from Oxford University and is well known as a speaker and writer on brand strategy, brand valuation, licensing, and marketing ROI issues.

Kelly Walsh

As MD Consumer Marketing, Kelly acts as senior client counsel on global/Western European equity development and credentialing strategies, with a particular focus on influencer marketing and stakeholder engagement. Over the past 7 years, Kelly has had extensive experience working as part of Integrated marketing communications teams for clients including Coca-Cola Company, Philips, Beverage Partners Worldwide, and P&G.

In addition to her client work, she oversees the Food & Drink, Beauty & Luxury, Consumer Health and Consumer Lifestyle groups. In this role she has acted as senior strategic counsel for P&G Western Europe (beauty, femcare, and fabric care), Philips, Nestle, Beam Global Spirits & Wine, InBev and Novartis Consumer Healthcare. As deputy CEO, Kelly also has responsibility for the Insights & Planning, Creative and Digital communications practice across the agency.

Before joining MS&L, Kelly was Consumer and Business Communications Director for MacLaurin Hatch Group (now Trimedia Harrison Cowley) working with BSkyB, O2, The Jim Henson Company and EMAP Publishing. She also spent time client-side – 4 years as PR director EMEA for US fashion company, Gap building the brand in UK and launching into Germany and France, and 2 years as PR Manager for L'Oreal Paris and Garnier. Her past agency experience has involved her in brand building work for clients as diverse as Ben & Jerry's to Fortnum & Mason and The Automobile Association.

Kelly is a member of the PRCA and has acted as guest speaker at AMEC and PRCA conferences on influencer and integrated marketing. She has been practicing PR in the UK for over 15 years.

Kelly holds a degree in Business Administration, Marketing from Ryerson University, Toronto, Ontario, Canada.

1
Integrated Brand Marketing and Measuring Returns

Philip J. Kitchen

1 Introduction

In March, 2008, AMEC – the Association for Measurement and Evaluation of Communication – hosted a practitioner conference in London where the twin themes in the title were addressed by all speakers. The speakers were as follows:

- *Myself*, topic given above.
- *Jan Lindemann*, the then Global Managing Director of Interbrand. He addressed the topic of 'Building Brand Value Through Integrated Marketing'.
- *Peter Cain*, then CEO of Optimor, Millward Brown who addressed the topic of 'Marketing Mix Modelling and Return on Investment'.
- *The CEO* of World Vision who addressed the topic of 'How an Area Development Programme Works from an Integrated Perspective'.
- *The CEO* of Visit London who addressed how 'Integrated Approaches Improved London Tourism.'

The conference was very well attended with many practitioners from multinationals and UK-based businesses, together with agency personnel who work closely with these companies to develop, implement, and measure returns from creative integrated communication programmes. It was decided to publish an edited book based on the conference proceedings. It is now, however, 3 years later. During that time, media have expanded and further fragmented. Measuring returns has become more straightforward on-line via mobile, and more complex as many more channels (media) have proliferated. Consumers are more streetwise, savvy, and sophisticated. Markets have further demassified and fragmented. Real audiences are more smudged than ever before. Meanwhile, the world has passed through a major economic crisis – the worst since the Wall Street Crash – and its aftermath will be felt and paid for, over many years. Personalities in the conference have moved on to pastures new. Thus the shape and design and contributors to the book have changed. We now have the latest inputs from some of the major movers and shapers in the field of brand communication and measurement. It is likely that their thoughts and views expressed here will help shape the subject as we move into the second decade of the twenty-first century.

I offer a few comments before leaving the stage to allow the major actors to present their work.

2   Key Challenges

The key challenges facing today's marketing and brand managers concern the interface between *traditional* sales, marketing and communications and *new, interactive* sales, marketing and communication. These brand activities are focussed upon customers and prospects with the need to measure or show marketplace results. A few years, Don Schultz, in my view the guru of integrated marketing communications, spoke of *transitioning* from old to new ways of communicating, based upon the needs associated with the new world of the twenty-first century (see Table 1.1). How does the firm or brand move from where they are now to where they need to be

Table 1.1   The old and the new approaches to integrated communications

The Old 'Traditionality'	The New – Twenty-first Century
1. Everything is outbound	1. Interactivity
2. Functional focus	2. Processes
3. National orientation	3. Global – every company
4. Tangible assets	4. Intangible
5. USP's	5. Customer value
6. Corporate monoliths	6. Alliances and affiliations
7. Communication as an option	7. Leading with [integrated] communications
8. Brands and branding	8. Branding absolutely core

in this dynamic global marketplace, The old 4P's (product, price, promotion, place) approach was essentially outbound, linear, and driven by a supply orientation. The reality is, of course, that markets are not, and perhaps never have been, product-, production-, or even marketing-driven. Now, more than ever before, markets are driven by customers, consumers, and prospects...and *all economies* pace businesses *will eventually be customer-dominated and customer-driven*. The business that really understands its customers and works with them, with the recognisance that business is demand-driven, should have (if approached correctly) an enormous source of ongoing information that should underpin competitive advantage. In the Kitchen and Schultz (2000) book *Raising the Corporate Umbrella*, we wrote two approaches, or mentalities that seemed to govern old or new approaches to integrated marketing and corporate brand communications....

In the twenty-first century just to play the marketing game requires supply side excellence. However, 'playing' is insufficient. Harold Abrahams when he lost a short sprint against Eric Lidell, in preparation for the 1924 Olympic Games, said 'I do not run to participate. I run to win!' Winning the marketing game in the twenty-first century requires demand-side excellence as well. This means staying close to customers, understanding their needs, communicating effectively, consistently and well. Businesses that do not do this, and exercise understanding of the dynamics facing their business, and adapt accordingly, *will fail*.

In 1983, the great marketer Theodore Levitt asked, what is the purpose of business?

> To get and keep a customer. Without solvent customers in some reasonable proportions, there is no business. Customers are constantly presented with lots of options to help them solve their problems. They don't buy things; they buy solutions to problems. *The surviving and thriving business is a business that constantly seeks better ways to help people solve their problems.* To create betterness requires knowledge of what customers think betterness to be. *This precedes all else in business* (Levitt, 1983). The imagination that figures out what that is, imaginatively figures out what should be done, and does it with imagination and high spirits will drive the enterprise forward (italics added).

Category	UK %	7 nations %	% change '04 v '01
Media advertising	40	40	0.7
Sales promotion	60	21	3.5
Brand PR/sponsorship	15	15	6.8
Direct mail	20	14	4.6
Interactive marketing	8	8	29.8

Figure 1.1   The challenge of digitalisation: A dramatic switch

Source: London Business School, Marketing Expenditure Trends, www.london.edu/marketing/met Used with permission.

Hence, customer insight and integrated brand marketing strategy are keys to winning the marketing game, a game fought in every country, and in every market, all over the world.

One major challenge in the twenty-first century is that of digitalisation, as was pointed out by a significant report produced by London Business School (2005).

Figure 1.1 shows relative stasis for media advertising across seven nations with growth for sales promotion, and brand PR/sponsorship and direct mail. However, interactive marketing shows massive growth. In 2010, we can see a resurgence of media advertising, growth for Brand PR, and sponsorship faltering in the face of a global downturn. Sales promotion (brand equity not price related) and direct mail will continue to show good performance, despite the latter's 'nuisance value'. Interactive marketing via three screens (TV, computer, and mobile) will likely dominate most media campaigns for the foreseeable future. Personalised, directable, measurable communications aimed at, and presumably for you and me. The situation varies depending upon company and market type as shown in Figure 1.2:

Media budget spend	B2B %	B2C %
Media advertising	30	50
Sales promotion	22	20
Brand PR/sponsorship	23	10
Direct mail	15	14
Interactive marketing	10	6

Figure 1.2 The challenge of digitalisation in the twenty-first century
Source: London Business School, Marketing Expenditure Trends, www.london.edu/marketing/met Used with permission.

This mix of brand communication tools varies by company and customer type. It may not be too soon to say that advertising will enjoy a massive resurgence in B2C in the next decade. There will be more delivery mechanisms, more opportunities, and lower prices. I firmly expect that integrated brand communications will be spearheaded by three-screen advertising, interactivity and marketing PR (other tools will play a lesser role). However, campaigns must have at their core ongoing knowledge regarding specific target markets. No knowledge, no data, will rapidly turn communications to solipsistic voices shouting in a wind tunnel.

The road to integration of messages is now complete, as the ideal of one-voice, one-sight, one-sound has become the standardised norm. What started as a single track, in 1993, has now become a super-highway for all companies. However, the journey towards integration from a consumer perspective has scarcely begun. Thus, what Don Schultz and I (2000) regarded as a four-stage process, for *the majority of companies*, has to all intents and purposes stalled at its very beginning. Message integration – Yes! Consumer integration – No! Most companies carry out poor ineffectual market research, or none at all. There is an insufficiency of real understanding of markets, marketplaces, or marketspaces. Most messages are still outbound and linear, with the added virtue of looking or sounding the same via all media. Integrated brand marketing, where one measures behavioural outcomes in response to marketing communication, is still a far-fetched and futuristic dream for most companies. As we see later in the chapters, there are techniques, processes, and workable techniques for after the event evaluation of integrated brand marketing, but virtually none that work with immediacy.

The decade spanning the millennial divide was the decade that witnessed the development and dominance of integrated marketing communications (IMC) albeit in terms of the one-voice phenomenon. In 2010, many organisations, in the same terms, consider IMC to be a key competitive advantage. However, IMC is in the midst of critical review. Many businesses and the agencies that service their communications needs are enmeshed in the first stage of development. The promise that IMC offered is fading. The reason why is that organisations took it seriously enough until associated costs started to rise. Now, only serious market downturn or negative actions by customers will force companies to take a different path.

Thus, there is a return on investment elephant in the room. Like the blind men of Industan who only identified the beast in part, we can say . . . .

So far as return on investment is concerned:

- It is a major area of criticism.
- Most companies are unwilling or perhaps unable to move beyond existing measurement tools and devices to any form of behavioural segmentation and associated measurement techniques.
- Behavioural measurement is dependent on understanding market dynamics, impossible without ongoing data and knowledge inputs.
- The issue of measurement and evaluation will continue to bedevil and/or will forestall future development of IMC.

However, a more realistic picture of IMC is *gradually* emerging from the maelstrom of debate, conceptualisation, and currently available evidence. The reality seems to be that IMC is situation-specific *and* context-dependent. While IMC is a widely accepted model and paradigm, actual use depends on what clients want and need in terms of communications.

IMC is current parlance in practitioner language and academic usage. However, if it is to be anything more than 'one-sight, one sound' orchestration of tactical promotion mix elements, then serious evidence of progression and use needs to be shown.

A further *and major* stumbling block to IMC is its marked inability to measure or evaluate outcomes. While one may liken successful outcome to the search for the Holy Grail, the technology, skills, models, and embryonic tools are available to move evaluation to the forefront and indeed forerunner in terms of IMC progression.

Difficult questions. IMC, in terms of its major tenets, design, contribution, and benefits, has gained academic and, as evidenced here, practitioner acceptance throughout the world. One can already make out the bones of what could be termed a 'central theory' which most IMC researchers and practitioners would accept. Around the edges (i.e. of PR, of turf battles, of a stages theory of IMC etc), there will be always be healthy disagreement, conjecture, and criticism. IMC has already proved to be remarkably robust; it is no passing phase or passing fad. However, the time has come for *more evidence* to be presented from client practitioners and for more sophisticated questions to be asked and answered. Only then, will the theoretical framework be strengthened. Current barriers seem eminently capable of being understood, corrected, and overcome.

The crucible of practice, where IMC was born and grew, is the crucible where IMC has undergoing change to integrated *brand marketing*. Evaluating brand marketing, rather than just communication or promotion, is a significant step forward, and one that can and will be justified in the following chapters. But still, we are missing something or someone, namely, customer and consumers. Perhaps some future book will be titled 'integrated brand consumer marketing' and include the required devices to measure during and after campaigns in the short, medium, and long term. Then we will see the fulfilment of both branding and marketing. For the latter, it will have taken the long road.

References

Kitchen, P.J. and Schultz, D.E. (2000) *Raising the Corporate Umbrella: Corporate Communications in the 21st Century*, Basingstoke, Palgrave-Macmillan.

Levitt, T. (1983) *The Marketing Imagination*, New York, The Free Press.

London Business School (2005) *Marketing Expenditure Trends*, www.london.edu/marketing/met. Used with permission. Accessed 21 November 2009.

2
Brand Valuation and IMC

Joanna Seddon

1 Introduction

Pressure on marketers to demonstrate the value of their activities has been growing over the last 10 years, intensified by the 2008 recession. At the same time that the demand for marketing accountability increased, achieving it has become more difficult. The fragmentation of media and growth of integrated marketing has created new challenges for both marketing strategy and its measurement.

There is an urgent need for an approach which not only measures the financial impact of marketing, but does so across an ever-widening spectrum of marketing initiatives. The objective of this chapter is to show how brand valuation tools and techniques can be applied to meet this need. Brand valuation has the potential to play a key integrating function, bringing other forms of measurement down to the same level and create a common currency for measurement.

To this end, this chapter will examine the origins and evolution of brand valuation. We will look at the different methodologies currently in use for valuing brands and the standards and rules governing brand valuation. The steps and data requirements for conducting a best practices brand valuation will be explained.

Examples will be given of the different applications for which brand valuation can be used – financial, strategic and measurement/management. This will be followed by an explanation of how marketing professionals can apply brand valuation techniques in their measurement of different types of marketing communications, and indicate the potential for using brand valuation to create the key linkages in an integrated marketing measurement system.

2   The growing demand for brand valuation and marketing accountability

Over the last 10 years, there has been a growing focus on the value of brand and marketing, both within the marketing community and outside it. The sources of this increased interest lie outside marketing and relate to changes in the underlying structure of industries and economies.

At the macro-level, the root cause is the shift from a manufacturing-led to service- and information-based economies, which started in the United States, but has since spread globally, with even China now affected. This has dramatically changed the financial structure of corporations. In the old manufacturing world, corporate value was a tangible value – the value contained in property, plant and equipment. These things were relatively easy to measure. This was the world for which the current accounting and financial valuation standards were created (mostly in the 1950s). They made sense until quite recently. As late as 1980, 80 percent of the value of the Fortune 500 was represented by tangible assets. Since then, change has happened fast. Intangible assets grew to overtake tangibles as a proportion of shareholder value around 1990. They now account for over 70 percent of the value of the S&P 500, and despite a blip in the 2008 crash, trending upwards (see Figure 2.1).

While there are many different types of intangible assets – for example, Microsoft has technology, Pfizer its R&D pipeline – for most companies, the most important intangible asset is brand. Millward Brown Optimor's analysis, drawing on BrandZ, the world's largest brand equity database, has determined that between a quarter and a third of global corporate value can be attributed to brand. This change in the structure of corporate assets has attracted the attention of accountants, corporate finance and tax authorities. Increasingly, they now understand the value of brands and are grappling to develop standard ways of measuring it (with varying degrees of success – see discussion below). This trend has not reversed, but been accelerated by the recession, as the value of many traditional assets (among them sub-prime loans and car plants) has evaporated.

At the corporate level, a shift in the nature of competition has made it impossible for even the most stubborn CEOs, CFOs and boards to ignore the importance of brand and marketing. In today's

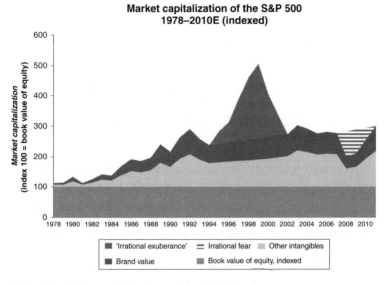

Figure 2.1   Market capitalization of the S&P 500

Source: Bloomberg, BrandZ, MB Optimor analysis.

business, the world is 'flat' – technology advances mean almost instant communications, everything is global, almost any new idea can be quickly copied. The traditional sources of competitive advantage, such as first mover in innovation, size and scale, labor cost and availability, have all but disappeared. As other things become equal, the only remaining differentiator is brand. It is not only Western corporations that realize this. The Chinese government, acutely aware that its low cost advantage was temporary, issued a decree urging Chinese businesses to build global brands as early as 2005, setting up a special government department to provide advice on how to do it, together with subsidies for brand development.

Increasingly, brand is on the table in mergers and acquisitions. Companies are being bought and sold for the brand asset, rather than any of the fixed assets. So, for example, when the Indian conglomerate Tata bought Jaguar and Land Rover in 2008, it was the two iconic brands they were paying $2 billion for, not the Ford production facilities.

Greater recognition of the importance of brand and marketing has brought with it a new emphasis on effectiveness. In the 1980s and

1990s it was all about the supply chain. The attention of managers and consultants was directed to squeezing costs out and maximizing supply chain efficiencies. By 2000, this was just about played out. Attention turned to the demand side, the spotlighted switched to marketing. Marketers have had to adjust the way they think and behave in response to the growing pressure for accountability. In a recent study conducted by Millward Brown for the 4As, marketers identified 'ROI/accountability' as their biggest marketing challenge. Accountability even beat 'limited resources' as marketer's biggest headache.

The search for greater marketing measurement has only intensified during the recession. More surprisingly, notwithstanding the short-term pressures, there is a move away from purely short-term measures, such as sales response modeling, and a growing demand for approaches that can integrate the quantification of short-term sales impacts with longer-term brand effects. The recession has made it clear that a focus on short-term marketing impacts may be more likely to sink than save a company. A comparison between General Motors and Toyota is telling. GM concentrated almost exclusively on short-term promotional activities (such as offering everyone an employee discount). While these activities worked, that is, they did

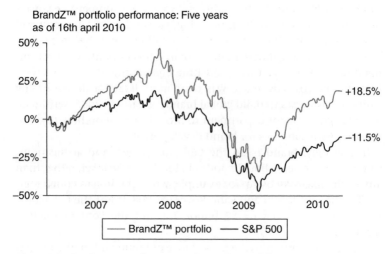

Figure 2.2   Stock price performance of BrandZ portfolio vs. S&P 500

grow short-term sales, the benefits were outweighed by the longer-term damage done to the value of the brand. Toyota, meanwhile, maintained its emphasis on brand building, and has been able to sell more cars, at lower discounts, than GM. Millward Brown Optimor's analysis, based on the BrandZ Top 100 most valuable brands, shows that companies which invest in building their brands are able to maintain higher share prices in a recession, and emerge with a sustainable competitive advantage when things improve (see Figure 2.2).

The outcome is a growing acceptance that short-term metrics are not enough – brand valuation has an important role to play in capturing the total value created by marketing.

3 The origins and evolution of brand valuation

Brand valuation is approximately 20 years old. The idea originated in the United Kingdom in the 1980s, following a wave of takeovers of consumer packaged goods companies: Keebler was bought by United Biscuits, Rowntree by Nestle and Pillsbury by Grand Metropolitan. The acquirers in each case paid a significant premium over the tangible assets on the balance sheet, which they were clear was for the intangible value of the brands. However, since intangibles couldn't be recognized on the balance sheet, these acquisitions created large amounts of goodwill, and led either to large amortization charges on the P&L or large write offs. The frustration surrounding this sparked a debate about how to quantify the value of brands in an acquisition. This focused on how to separate out the amount paid for the brand from the total amount of goodwill. The first internal valuation of a brand followed in the United Kingdom in 1988, when Rank Hovis McDougall (RHM) successfully used a valuation of its portfolio of brands in its defence against a hostile takeover bid by Goodman Fielder Wattie (GFW). This demonstrated that it was possible to value internally generated brands as well as brands being acquired. Following this, in 1989 the London Stock Exchange approved the inclusion of intangible assets in the asset classes used for shareholder approval in takeovers, and UK companies, including Grand Metropolitan, Guinness and Ladbrokes, rushed to put the value of brands they had bought on their balance sheets.

The motivation for the first brand valuations was thus acquisition accounting. The approaches used were somewhat simplistic. The value of a brand was defined as the difference in value between a branded product and an unbranded or generic product. While the concept is clearly sound, this approach is almost impossible to implement systematically. In most industries there just aren't enough generic products for comparison – all products and services are branded. Even in consumer packaged goods, where the concept originated, there are few generic products left – the 'own-label' products of supermarkets such as Sainsbury and Tesco are now brands in their own right. At the time, this didn't matter so much. Valuations were conducted solely for the purpose of recording the number to gain accounting and tax advantages. Although the companies valuing their brands recognized that there was a more serious concept behind this – the idea that brands are value-adding assets – there was no thought of actively managing the value of brand assets. Instead, there was almost an obsession with the idea of 'putting brands on the balance sheet'. A widespread myth developed that this was the sole purpose of brand valuation, which did much to hinder its broader application.

The next development was the adoption of brand value as a brand metric for internal purposes. The idea was that this represented a step forward in brand measurement. A financial number for the brand was seen as a superior metric to market research-based brand metrics. Almost every large company at some time or other has conducted an internal brand valuation exercise which delivered a brand value number for each division as well as for the company as a whole. In some cases (e.g., AT&T, Samsung Electronics), these numbers have been used as Key Performance Indicators (KPIs), where size of management bonuses is impacted by brand value growth. In principle, this is an excellent idea. The problem has been lack of transparency. The method used, by Interbrand and others, has been based almost exclusively on financial data. This was taken away, put into a 'black box' and numbers spat out. The most critical piece of information needed to determine brand value – the contribution of brand to total business value – was estimated on the basis of qualitative management interviews and work sessions. We would argue that this approach is not only open to abuse, but also of very limited usefulness. If the drivers through which brand value is created are not calculated in a robust fashion, there is no possibility of understanding how brand value is created. The output is limited to a set of numbers, which, as business circumstances change, rapidly become meaningless.

There has been growing interest in externally published rankings of brand values in the last 5 years. While brand rankings have been around, on and off since 1995, their popularity has increased with the emergence of Millward Brown Optimor and the *Financial Times* as a counterpart to Interbrand and *Business Week*. The rankings are important because they draw the attention of CEOs, CFOs and the financial community to the fact that brands have value, and in some cases, a great deal of value. Millward Brown Optimor's BrandZ Top 100 brands were together worth $2 trillion in 2009, a number which is equal to the GDP of Italy; the world's most valuable brand, Google, is by itself worth over $100 billion. Millward Brown Optimor's ranking includes all the components of a robust brand valuation. The only difference between the ranking and a strategic brand valuation exercise, conducted to identify how to grow the value of an individual client's brand or brands, is the depth of analysis. Since hundreds of brands are valued, the BrandZ ranking is obviously less detailed. The BrandZ Top 100 combines financial data, from Bloomberg, with detailed product and market information from Data Monitor, and brand equity data, from BrandZ. BrandZ is the world's largest brand equity study, conducted annually by Millward Brown for WPP. It includes over 50,000 brand measurements, conducted across 30 countries, 433 categories and more than 1 million consumers and business customers, over the last 10 years (see Figure 2.3).

The BrandZ Top 100 differs from the *Business Week* ranking in several key respects. The major difference is that it is based on financial data, and the key metric of the brand contribution to financial value is derived from quantitative data about the strength of the brands, rather than internal estimates. In addition, the BrandZ ranking values market facing brands, not corporate brands. So, for example, the valuation of Coca Cola includes only the three 'My Coke' brands (Coca Cola, Coca Cola Diets and Lites, and Coke Zero); other brands such as Sprite, Minute Maid, Dasani and so on owned by The Coca Cola Company are valued separately. Purely corporate brands such as Procter & Gamble and Unilever are not included. Finally, the BrandZ ranking is much more comprehensive in its geographical and industry

Global rank	Brand	Brand value ($m)
1	Google	114,260
2	IBM	86,383
3	(Apple)	83,153
4	Microsoft	76,344
5	Coca-Cola	67,983
6	M	66,005
7	Marlboro	57,047
8	中国移动通信 CHINA MOBILE	52,616
9	GE	45,054
10	vodafone	44,404

MillwardBrown Optimor

Figure 2.3   BRANDZ™ top 100 most valuable brands 2009

coverage than other rankings. The valuation is built up brand by brand, country by country, by industry category.

More robust approaches are now being applied not only to externally published rankings, but also to brand valuation tools used for internal brand measurement. These allow more of the potential for brand valuation as a measurement tool to be realized. The secret is to make the non-financial inputs to brand valuation as reliable as possible, basing them not on judgment but on the statistical analysis of quantitative market research data. The objective is to equal or surpass the robustness of the financial metrics (which, given the fact that financial valuations are based on forecasts, is not as far-fetched as it may seem). A brand valuation which incorporates quantitative market research and industry data delivers best-in-class brand assessment and a broader array of brand metrics, including:

- Brand financial value, overall and for each segment included in the valuation
- The contribution of brand to financial value
- Brand effectiveness in driving value by customer touch point
- Benchmarking of brand strength and effectiveness versus competitors.

A robust brand value analysis is the precondition for the use of brand valuation as a strategic tool. The primarily financial approach to brand valuation taken by older practitioners, such as Interbrand and Brand Finance, may meet the needs of finance professionals for compliance or royalty rate determination or of management for benchmark metrics, but is of little use for running the business.

The newer approach to brand valuation, used by Millward Brown Optimor and some other consulting firms, is more strategic. The view is that brand valuation should not be just about a number. Properly applied, the brand valuation approach can be used not just to measure the current value that brand contributes to a business, but also to identify the strategies and actions that the company can take to grow that value. This 'shareholder value-added' approach transforms brand valuation into a strategic tool for brand and marketing, introducing accountability into the management of one of the company's most valuable assets.

The latest development in strategic brand value management is the extension of brand valuation tools to marketing communications management. On its own, the brand valuation tool is sufficient to address the 'big picture' marketing issues, identifying the products, markets and customer segments where investment in brand will have the most impact. However, traditional brand valuation approaches do not provide answers to questions concerning the allocation of integrated marketing communications (IMC) budgets across different types of activity, such as on-line and off-line advertising, promotions, sponsorship and events, social media and others. This requires an additional step. Later on in this chapter we show how data on different types of marketing impacts, including both direct sales response impacts and indirect brand impacts, can be linked into the brand valuation model to create a common currency for measurement.

4 Examination of different brand valuation approaches

There are a number of different methodologies in common use for valuing brands. Six distinctly different approaches can be identified. These can be classified into three categories: External, Incomplete and Internal. The key characteristics of each are illustrated in Figure 2.4:

EXTERNAL		
1. Market based	Value of the brand is determined from comparable transactions	Limited. Useful for calculating norms and as a check upon other forms of valuation
2. Royalty relief		
INCOMPLETE		
3. Cost based	Each examines one aspect of how a brand creates value	Flawed. Should not be used on their own to value brands.
4. Price premium		
5. Brand equity		
INTERNAL		
6. Economic use	Measures a number of aspects of how a brand creates value	Best practices. However, implementation varies in robustness and comprehensiveness

Figure 2.4 Commonly used methodologies for valuing brands

4.1 'External' Brand Valuation Methodologies

The first category of brand valuation methods is classified as 'External' because the valuation is derived from analysis of the market in which the brand operates rather than of the business which is branded. The objective is to put a value on a brand at one given point in time. The focus is on deriving a means to get to a number. These valuation methods provide no insight into the sources of brand value, or guidance on how to manage the brand. They can be useful for financial purposes but are not applicable to brand or business management. They are typically geared toward transactions, such as mergers and acquisitions, brand securitization or licensing deals (internal or external). They are also often used for the purpose of reporting brands on balance sheets, as required by accounting rules. Because these methods are static in nature, and are relatively unsophisticated, they are often referred to as 'back-of-the-envelope approaches'.

The concept is that a brand can be valued by comparison to other brands whose value has been established in the marketplace. Key metrics used for valuing the brand are taken from third-party examples, using publicly available data. These approaches are based on the assumption that it is possible to find sufficient information on comparable transactions to deduce parameters to apply to the brand being valued.

There are two valuation approaches which fall into this category: the market-based method, and the royalty relief method.

4.1.1 Comparables – Market-based valuations

At its most simple, this method consists of taking disclosed brand values for comparable brands, and applying those to the brand being valued. A more sophisticated approach consists of using brand valuation multiples.

If there are transactions available that actually disclose a specific value for the brand, one can then calculate a multiple for that transaction – say brand value per Euro of revenue, or brand value per Euro of EBITDA, and then apply that multiple to the brand being valued.

The problem with comparables is that relevant data is often not available. First, it is very difficult, and often impossible, to find truly comparable brand transactions. Secondly, in most cases, available transactions do not specifically disclose brand values but just overall enterprise values. It then becomes necessary to estimate what portion of the enterprise value is related to the brand being valued and then apply a multiple to that value. This is particularly difficult in cases where a company operates with more than one brand, and in more than one country. Without access to internal data, value cannot be accurately attributed to a brand.

In the end, it often turns out that the only validation of the available data is that it resulted in a transaction, that is, that it was accepted as fair by both sides. For these reasons, the multiple approach is generally used as a secondary methodology, to test and validate the results obtained from other brand valuation methods, just as one would check a company valuation against market valuation multiples of comparable companies.

4.1.2   *Royalty relief*

The royalty relief method arrives at the value of a brand by calculating the value of the future royalty payments that a company would need to pay a third party to license the brand, if it did not own the brand itself. A royalty rate is applied to forecast future sales. The stream of brand royalties is then discounted back to a net present value.

The problem then becomes how to determine what would be the correct royalty fee levels for the brand, especially in the case when the brand to be valued is not already licensed out. Here, the most common approach is to look at licensing deals for comparable brands. Licensing databases with information on past transactions are available for this purpose.

This approach is market based: The valuation is based on what the market would be willing to pay for a license to the brand. For this reason, this approach is often favored by accounting firms, since market value is an accepted test of a fair valuation by most accounting standards.

The problem with this approach is that the brand licensing market lacks transparency and sophistication. The first comparable was usually established by rule of thumb. Comparables reflect the balance of power between particular licensors and licensees at the time of negotiation rather than the intrinsic value of the brand. As a result, valuations based on royalty relief calculations tend to undervalue the brand and favor the licensee over the licensor, as no business-related rationale was provided to justify royalty rates. For this reason, there is a growing trend in brand licensing away from pure comparables-based analysis to an income-based approach, which combines comparables analysis with metrics relating to the particular brand's effectiveness in driving value.

4.2   Incomplete Brand Valuation methodologies

Certain brand valuation approaches are fundamentally flawed in their logic. The main issue is that they only look at one aspect of brand value. When used in isolation, these methods fail the most basic test of any valuation method: that it should be conceptually sound. However, when used in conjunction with other methods, they can provide a useful check and throw additional light on specific sources of brand value.

Three such approaches are in common usage: the cost-based approach, the premium price method and the brand equity approach.

4.2.1 Cost-based approaches

The idea is that a brand can be valued as the sum of the marketing and advertising costs incurred to build the brand, or of the replacement cost if the brand had to be built from scratch today.

This approach has two major flaws. First, it assumes that future value can be related to past costs, which is not necessarily the case. Spending has never been a guaranteed way to build value. There are numerous examples of companies who have spent millions or even billions on advertising without creating a strong brand.

The most extreme cases occurred during the dot-com boom. In 2000 Internet businesses are estimated to have spent over $3 billion on TV and sponsorships. Today, most of these brands have disappeared. Perhaps the best-known example is Pets.com, the on-line pet food delivery business, which spent over $47.5 million in advertising in 2 years including a $2 million Super bowl spot featuring its famous sock puppet, before collapsing in November 2000. After the company folded, the rights to the puppet were sold, for just $125,000. Other dotcoms committed themselves to multi-year stadium sponsorships, which they then had to renege on, amid extreme embarrassment. Webvan, an on-line grocery delivery service, undertook a 3-year sponsorship of the San Francisco ballpark, at a cost of several million dollars. This included putting Webvan stickers on the stadium's 43,000 cup holders (which had to be peeled off soon after when the company went bust). Other stadiums had to be ignominiously renamed. These included not only the Houston Astro's Enron field, a $100 million, 30-year deal (the sponsorship has been resold, back to an old economy brand and the stadium was renamed Minute Maid), but also the New England Patriots CMGI stadium (a 15-year $114 million sponsorship) and the Baltimore Ravens' PSINet Stadium). More traditional businesses have also paid out huge sums on advertising without producing commensurate results. SBC and Bell South launched Cingular as the brand for their wireless telephony joint venture in May 2001, with huge fanfare and a Super Bowl ad. In the next 5 years, they paid out over $4 billion advertising on Cingular but failed to create a strong bond with consumers. In 2007, SBC bought Bell South and rushed to kill the brand, announcing its replacement by AT&T 3 weeks later.

The second fallacy of the cost-based approach is that it presupposes that brands are built only through investment in advertising – whereas as we all know, brand is the result of many different types of investment: not only advertising and marketing, but also R&D and product design, and every aspect of the customer experience. Starbucks and Google are two companies which created valuable brands, without significant investment in marketing. Starbuck's brand was built almost wholly by investment in the coffee shop experience. Its advertising spend ran at less than 1 percent of revenues through 2007. Only from 2008, as the experience and sales declined, did Starbucks turn to advertising, still spending a fraction of that of rivals such as McDonalds. Google has overtaken its rivals and built the world's most valuable brand by focusing relentlessly on an ever more user-friendly experience, not by investing in advertising. During 2003–2008 advertising investment was 1/10 that of AOL, MSN and Yahoo. In 2008, Google's off-line advertising was a mere $25 million, of which $11.6 million was spent on recruiting.

Cost-based approaches can be helpful as a 'rule of thumb' for allocating ownership when more than one party has invested in marketing a brand. However, even in these cases, measurement of the comparative effectiveness of their marketing initiatives needs to be taken into account.

4.2.2   Price premium

The idea behind the price premium method is that a brand creates value by enabling its owner to charge a premium price for the products sold under that brand name. The method then consists of estimating that price premium based on a study of non-branded products in the category, or of market research on price sensitivity and purchase behavior. A brand price premium is then calculated and applied to estimates of future sales volumes, and brand cash flows are calculated and then discounted to arrive at a brand value.

The fundamental flaw of this approach is the initial hypothesis, that brands create value only by being able to charge a price premium. In reality, brands create value in a given category by any superior combination of a price premium and a volume premium. In the case of a high-end fashion brand such as Louis Vuitton for instance, there is a very high price premium, offset by a negative volume premium: there are more unbranded suitcases sold than Vuitton luggage. In the case of discount brands such as Wal-Mart, for instance, it is exactly the opposite: There is a negative price premium more than offset by a positive volume premium. For both of these types of brands, the premium price approach would fail to provide an accurate valuation.

In some highly commoditized categories, brand owners may feel that price premium is the most meaningful measure of brand health. Hewlett Packard, for example, has utilized the price premium approach. However, it must be recognized that this is only part of the answer. Unless price premium is used in combination with an approach that also takes volume into consideration, it will provide an inaccurate reflection of brand value.

4.2.3 Brand equity 'valuation' approaches

Some methods attempt to calculate a brand value without any connection to the financials of the business they are considering. Underlying this is confusion over the exact meaning of the words 'brand value'. This phrase is sometimes used as if it were interchangeable with the term 'brand equity'. Brand equity is itself a rather vague and imprecise term. It is most generally used to denote a brand proposition and set of attributes, intended to differentiate a company's products and services from competitors and create a bond with its customers.

Market research companies have developed different techniques for measuring brand equity. Some of these focus on brand attributes and personality, others consider the customers' relationship with the brand. An example of the attribute-based approach is Y&R's Brand Asset Valuator. This measures the strength of brand perceptions along four dimensions: Differentiation, Relevance, Esteem and Knowledge. BAV also evaluates Brand Image using a mix of 48 'image' and 'personality' attributes. Millward Brown's Brand Dynamics methodology measures a brand's success in converting its customers of its products into loyal or 'bonded' customers. It recognizes that in all markets, a small number of consumers account for a large proportion of sales. Loyal customers are more valuable to a brand than occasional customers. The Brand Dynamics pyramid measures the stages through which a customer relationship develops and quantifies the brand's success in creating loyalty. The Brand Signature identifies a brand's strengths and weaknesses at each level. Brand Voltage, a summary of signature, is a leading indicator of share (see Figure 2.5).

Similar frameworks based on 'the customer funnel' are also used in by some of the management consulting companies, for example, McKinsey. Another way to build Economic Use valuation models without link to business financials is through correlation of brand metrics with stock performance, the method preferred by CoreBrand. The idea here is to find out how much of the company's market capitalization can be accounted for by brand-related factors – the approach, however, is purely external, includes no business valuation and has very poor granularity.

All of these brand equity approaches only provide part of the answer. Market research is an important component of any brand valuation methodology that seeks to understand how brand drives value. However, on its own, the answers provided by research stop at 'abstract' attributes, such as 'image', 'consideration' and 'loyalty'. A hard financial component must be added to determine the financial value of the brand.

Of these research methodologies, the 'pyramid' or 'customer funnel' approaches, which measure customer relationships, are best

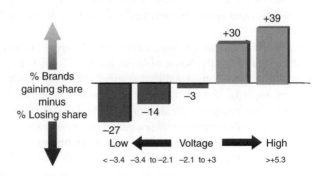

Figure 2.5 Voltage validated by market share analysis

adapted to brand valuation. Attempts have been made to link image-based approaches, as Y&R's Brand Asset Valuator (BAV), to business financials, with little success. The most serious of these, Brand Economics, a joint venture of Young & Rubicam and the EVA consultants Stern Stewart, has now gone out of business.

On their own, all purely research-based methodologies are inadequate. There is no direct connection to shareholder value, and brand measurement is not integrated with company financials.

4.3   Internal or 'Economic Use' brand valuation methodologies

The preferred method for valuing brands is the Economic Use approach. If properly implemented, Economic Use brand valuation combines the best elements of the financial market approaches (hard financial numbers) with the advantages of the brand equity-based approaches (research-based measurement of customer attitudes toward brands). Economic Use brand valuation can provide both a robust financial value for the brand and an understanding of how brand creates value in the business. This makes it possible to identify the actions which can be taken to grow the value which brand adds to the business. Brand valuation ceases to be just a brand measurement tool and becomes a brand management tool.

The Economic Use approach is focused on looking internally, inside the business which owns and uses the brand. It quantifies the financial returns created as a result of this brand exploitation.

Underlying the brand valuation is a financial valuation of the business. This conforms to accounting standards for valuation and is similar to valuation approaches used by analysts and accountants. This is most commonly either a Discounted Cash Flow (DCF) or Economic Profit approach, though other valuation methodologies can also be used (e.g., in financial services, an equity-based valuation is required). In all cases, the valuation is based on an analysis of historical financial results and a forecast of future performance. The difference between the DCF and Economic Profit approaches is that in a DCF valuation, it is future cash flows that are forecasted; while an Economic Profit valuation is based on future projections of earnings (for this reason, it is also often called an 'Income' approach).

Future cash flows or earnings streams are forecasted for each part of the business, just as in a standard business valuation. An additional piece of analysis is then conducted to identify a portion of free cash flows or earnings which can reasonably be attributed to brand. This is known as the 'Brand Contribution' or 'Role of Brand' analysis. It can take several different forms, some based on estimation, others more robust. The preferred approach (a guide to which appears later in this chapter) is to conduct statistical analysis of brand equity data.

The portion of cash flows or earnings that have been identified as driven by brand is then discounted back to a present value based on a risk factor of the brand's durability. The discount rate used is a multifactor approach (equivalent to financial beta models such as Fama-French) but incorporating brand risk–related factors, most commonly derived from benchmarking the brand's strength against competitors.

The advantages of the Economic Use approach are that, first, it is inherently more accurate than other methodologies, since it is based on data about the business using the brand, rather than, as in the External approaches, data about other brands. Secondly, it creates the possibility of drilling down into the drivers of brand value, allowing the sources of value to be identified. This means that it can be used not just as a financial tool, providing a point in time brand value number, but also as a management tool, to identify the strategies that will do most to grow the value that brand adds to the business. A robust Economic Use valuation sets up a model, into which marketing communications data can be linked, to provide a measurement of the total marketing impact on financial value and a means for optimizing short- and long-term spend.

5   Rules and standards pertaining to brand valuation

The number of rules and standards which touch on the measurement of brand and other intangibles has blossomed in the last 5 years. This is a direct reflection of the growth of importance of intangibles as a portion of shareholder value. Accountants, analysts and regulators can see that the world has changed and are struggling to come to grips with new forms of measurement that will introduce the same levels of accountability into intangible as exist for tangible asset management. As we will see, they have done this with varying degrees of success. While some of the rules and standards make sense, others are highly illogical, and many are extremely vague. They fall into three categories: Accounting, Tax and Operational standards.

5.1 The accountants' view of brand valuation

Since the late 1990s, changes in US and international accounting standards have led to a massive increase in the number of brand valuations conducted for balance sheet reporting and compliance purposes. As has been shown, the accounting profession's interest in the value of brands was sparked by difficulties of accounting for goodwill in the aftermath of a slew of brand acquisitions in the United Kingdom. The first accounting standard to regulate the ability to put brands on the balance sheet was introduced in 1985 through UK accounting standard SSAP 22. This allowed a choice of immediate write-off or gradual amortization of goodwill. Other countries followed suit, in a patchwork fashion – beginning with other Anglo-Saxon nations such as Australia and Canada, followed by other large economies, including France, Germany and Japan. The first step toward introduction of a consistent approach came in 1998 when the International Accounting Standards board (a primarily European body) issued two concurrent sets of guidelines, IAS 36 and 38. However, these were recommendations only – the board had no prescriptive power.

Two key turning points came in 2001 and 2002. The first was in 2001, when the US Financial Accounting Standards Board (FASB) which had long held out against regulation of intangibles, and innovation in accounting standards in general, issued SFAS 141 and 142, which made it possible to put acquired intangibles, including brands, on the balance sheets of US corporations. The second was in June 2002, when the European Union passed a regulation requiring European companies listed in EU securities markets to prepare their consolidated financial statements in accordance with the international standards, starting with the financial year 2005. The name IAS was changed to IFRS (International Financial Reporting Standards) to mark the regulations' new compulsory status. The change spurred convergence among accounting standards within the EU, and, from 2007 outside it, when the application of the IFRS rules was extended to cover non-EU companies with EU listings. As part of all this, the existing accounting standards for intangibles were revised in 2004 and an additional regulation, IFRS 3, was issued, updated again in 2008.

The two current sets of accounting rules for intangibles, IFRS and US GAAP, have much in common. Among the shared features:

- It is accepted that brands may have an indefinite life and do not have to be depreciated along with the remainder of goodwill.
- The value of brands which a company acquires may consequently be placed on the balance sheet.
- Regular impairment tests are required to measure the continuing appropriateness of the value of brands placed on the balance sheet.

There are minor differences in the application of these rules – in general the IFRS is slightly more favorable to the treatment of brands than US GAAP (see Figure 2.6). These differences are gradually disappearing, and will vanish entirely in future, with the planned extension of IFRS to the United States.

5.2   The tax authorities' view of brand valuation

The tax authorities, most notably the OECD and the US IRS, were quick to get wise to the tax implications of ways thought up by international businesses for the management of their brand assets. In their most advanced form, these include the creation of separate brand holding companies for the management of the brand asset. In this arrangement, ownership of the global brand is sold to the holding company, which is located in a low tax jurisdiction (Switzerland in the case of Shell and Nestle, Ireland for Vodafone, Delaware for a number of US corporations). The brand and certain brand management and marketing functions are then licensed back to the corporation's subsidiaries, in return for an annual royalty fee. The advantages for the corporation include more centralized brand management and control, greater appreciation by subsidiaries of the value of the brand (since they have to pay for it) and certain tax benefits. The IRS in particular was quick to jump on this as a means by

Relevant standards (revised January 2008)	
International • IFRS 3 (2008)	US • SFAS 141 (relating to acquisition accounting) • SFAS 142 (relating to impairment testing)
Key provisions	

1. Conditions under which intangible assets should be recognized on the balance sheet

- The acquirer should split intangibles out from good will and recognize them as assets on the balance sheet, when they meet certain criteria:
    - Separability. The intangible is separable when it can be split from the entity and sold or licensed out
    - Contractual-legal. If there are contractual or other legal rights involved, the intangible should be accounted for separately, even when it cannot be separated out from the entity

2. Classes of intangibles which should be considered for recognition

i) Marketing-related	Trademarks, trade names, service marks, trade dress (unique color, shape or package design), newspaper mastheads, internet domain names, non-competition agreements. A set of complementary assets commonly referred to as a brand can be recognized as a single asset.
ii) Customer-related	Customer lists, order or production backlogs, customer contract and customer relationships including non contractual relationships.
iii) Artistic-related	Plays, operas, ballets, books, magazines, newspapers, pictures photographs
iv) Contract-based	Licensing and royalty agreements, advertising, construction, service or supply agreements, lease agreements, franchising agreements, employment contracts.
v) Technology-based	Patented technology, computer software, unpatented technology (Know-how), databases, trade secrets such as formulas, processes and recipes.

3. How the intangibles should be valued

- When: as of the date that control passes to the new owners
- How: at fair market value. This is defined slightly differently by the two sets of standards:
- IFRS: Value in use to the owner　　　　–FASB: Market value i.e. value if sold

4. Measurement of changes in value

- Intangible assets should be tested for impairment annually (a one step process according to the IFRS, a two step assessment according to US GAAP (first screen for impairment, then measure the amount)
- Additional testing should be conducted between annual tests if an event occurs that would more likely than not reduce the fair value of a reporting below its carrying amount (IFRS only)
- Excess brand value is written off as a charge to profit (IFRS); taken as a reduction in asset value on the balance sheet (US GAAP)
- No increase in brand value allowed

Figure 2.6 Main features of the International and US GAAP accounting standards for intangibles

which US corporations export part of their US-generated earnings to lower tax jurisdictions, and brought law suits against companies such as DHL for this reason as early as the 1990s.

Today, there are a number of standards in place governing the calculation of brand licensing rates, as part of transfer pricing regulations. The largest body of standards is issued by the OECD. As with brand valuation, the European standards are mirrored by the US authorities, in this case the IRS.

Tax authorities treat internal brand royalty systems as a transfer pricing issue. A royalty is the price paid to get usage of an

	Comparable price (CUP)	Resale price (RPM)	Cost-plus (CPM)
Principle	Looks at prices charged for similar trademark rights in comparable uncontrolled transactions	Establishes the price a licensee should pay to allow it to earn a gross margin similar to that of companies in similar industries	Computed by multiplying the cost of designing & maintaining the trademark by an appropriate gross profit percentage to cover the functions it carries out
Practical considerations and challenges	Looking in "uncontrolled", i.e. external licensing transactions, licensor marketing support levels may be very different	Less applicable to brand licensing since the licensing fee would not be part of the gross margin calculation	It is difficult to allocate a cost of brand building to each licensee

Figure 2.7   Transaction-based 'Arms-Length' pricing methods for intangible assets

intangible good: The trademark. There are six approved transfer pricing methods, which can be divided into two types:

- Traditional transaction-based methods: Compare actual past transactions
- Profit-based methods: Look at the profitability of the involved entities.

The arm's-length standard applies to all methods: Pricing on a 'fair value basis'.

Transaction-based methods are based either on comparable prices or comparable costs (see Figure 2.7). In all cases the royalty rate is established by examining prior transactions of other companies.

Profit-based methods may be based on comparables or on actual financials. Comparable profits and transactional net margin methods utilize comparable profitability analysis. Profit split allocates the actual financial results of the business between the two parties (see Figure 2.8).

5.3   The operational standards bodies' view of brand valuation

International standards bodies have only recently got seriously involved in brand valuation. The initial impetus came from Germany in 2004, when a joint committee of accountants and brand valuation experts sponsored a study, in which nine different companies were asked to value the same brand and came up with nine different

	Comparable profits (CPrM)	Transactional net margin (TNMM)	Profit split (PSM)
Principle	Establishes the price a licensee should pay to allow it to earn operating margins similar to that of companies with similar operating model and size	Similar to CPrM, but looks at operating margins on a macro, company wide level rather than at a micro level	Looks at splitting indistinguishable (i.e. non licensee or licensor specific) profits between licensee and licensor based on either market or non-market based factors
Practical considerations and challenges	Relative to CUP, focuses more on operating model similarities (i.e. capital intensity, importance of intangibles, size, etc.), also looks at operating profit rather than gross margin, making it more applicable to brands	Is more practical than CPrM in some cases where data is hard to get; is therefore very popular	Considered a last resort method by the OECD several countries either do not accept PSM at all or they hold PSM to extreme transfer pricing scrutiny

Figure 2.8   Profit-based 'Arms-Length' pricing methods for intangible assets

answers. Following this, DIN, the German Institute for Standardization initiated a project which was taken up by the ISO, the International Standards Organization, for developing brand valuation standards. Technical Committee 231 has been working on the standard since March 2007. Standards organizations and committees of experts from 14 participating and four observing countries have been involved. The standard is in the final stages of discussion (ISO/DIS 10668), with the final publication date is expected to be in 2010.

The draft standard approves three brand valuation methods, all of which fit within the conceptual framework established by the OECD and other tax authorities (see Figure 2.9).

- Intrinsic (based on the actual value generated by the brand in the business)
- Comparable (based on prior transaction in the marketplace)
- Cost-based (based on past investments)

All these rules and standards represent a significant step forward in that they do at least recognize that intangibles can have value which investors and creditors should know about. However, they are still a very long way from reflecting the true value which particularly brands can add to a corporation.

The accounting standards are the most problematic. Both the IFRS and US GAAP rules are based on a principle, which is clearly illogical

	Income approach	Market approach	Cost approach
Description	Measures value of the brand based on the present value of the economic benefits generated over the remaining life of the brand	Measures value based on what other purchasers in market have paid for reasonably similar brands	Measures value of the brand based on the cost invested in building the brand, or its replacement, or reproduction cost
Practical considerations and challenges	Must estimate the expected after-tax cash flows attributable to the brand over its useful life and discount these to the present value using a discount rate	Straight brand value comparisons are hard to come by. May have to be adjusted for brand size or brand strength relative to competitors	Basically assumes that ROI on past expenses is equal to $1 per $ spent. Actual marketing ROIs can greatly vary
Similarities to OECD standards	By looking at the economic benefits of the brand, it rebalances profitability between licensee and licensor to reflect approaches such as RPM, CPrM and TNMM	Conceptually similar to the Comparable Uncontrolled Price method (CUP)	Somewhat similar to the Cost Plus Method (CPM), except it looks at costs only, without consideration of a profit margin or marketing ROI

Figure 2.9   ISO brand valuation approaches

(or in accounting parlance, 'asymmetrical'). Reporting requirements for intangible assets deal exclusively with those assets that have been acquired. This implements a distinction between internally generated brands and those acquired as part of a transaction. A company which buys a brand may have to value it and put it on its balance sheet, while it is not allowed to do the same for its own internally grown brand. Thus, when Coca Cola bought PowerAde, it had to value the brand and put it on its balance sheet, but is not able to reflect the value of the Coca Cola brand in its financial reporting, even though it is self-evident that the Coca Cola brand constitutes the majority of the value of the corporation. Another 'asymmetrical' feature is the fact that when brand value is retested each year, a fall in brand value has to be accounted for. However, there is no provision for recognizing brand value growth.

The tax and operational standards go a step further and attempt to describe approved methods for valuing brands. The intention – to introduce more consistency into brand valuation methods and ensure a certain level of quality – is clearly excellent. Recognition of the value of brands has been held back by the plethora of superficial valuation methodologies and the lack of a generally accepted and mandated approach. Unfortunately, in neither case do these standards do enough to redress the situation. Compiled by committees and heavily influenced by the accounting profession, they are very vague and all-inclusive. Methods included in the ISO standards, for example, include the valuation of brands on a cost basis, that is, to value the brand at the cost of the prior years' advertising spend, a clearly flawed approach, which in our opinion should not be used.

The extent to which the current financial rules place continued stress on tangible assets and tend to mislead investors can be seen from the case of Gillette. Gillette was bought by Procter & Gamble in 2005 for a price of $57 billion, when, according to its financials, the company only possessed $3 billion of asset value. Why did Procter & Gamble pay $54 billion over and above the apparent value of the business? Capitalizing the cost of advertising would not explain it (Gillette spent only $1.6 billion on advertising in 2004). What is Gillette's real asset? The brand loyalty of millions of customers, who buy one set of Gillette razor blades after another, over many decades of their lives. Investors, such as Warren Buffet, who were savvy enough to spot the extent to which Gillette's value was under-reported, reaped a bonanza (Buffet was paid $5.2 billion for the 96 million of Gillette shares he purchased for $600 million in 1989).

The tendency to under or overvalue brands has been compounded by the somewhat cavalier attitude to reporting brand value adopted by many of the large accounting firms. Brand valuation is too often regarded as a purely financial exercise, without involvement of marketing departments or corporate strategy, and consequently, without any thought for the future. A number of companies rushed to put brands at high values on their balance sheets when the 2001–2002 rules came in, seeking immediate tax benefits. The results can be dangerous and costly. Hewlett Packard's experience with Compaq provides an object lesson. In 2002 Hewlett Packard acquired the Compaq brand and put it on the balance sheet for a value of $1.422 billion. Since under FAS 141 and 142 it cannot be amortized, it remains there at just under 2 percent of the company's total assets. Meanwhile, Hewlett Packard has practically discontinued use of the Compaq brand, which is generating virtually no value. As a consequence, the company has been faced with a major tax issue and write-off.

The good news is that the people drawing up the standards are conscious of these issues, and that gradual steps are being taken to correct the anomalies. There is growing acceptance that the best definition of the value of brands is that based on an estimate of the future earnings they can generate.

6   Best practices in brand valuation – A step-by-step guide

Best practices brand valuations start from the idea that it is necessary to understand the sources of the value that brands generate for companies. Only then does the brand valuation have meaning as a tool for managing the value of the brand asset. Without an understanding of the sources of value, brand valuation is limited to being an exercise to produce a point-in-time number.

How do you measure the sources of brand value? The first step is to define brand, in a way that makes sense both to accountants and to brand managers. Technically, brand has two components:

$$\text{Brand} = \text{Identity} + \text{Reputation}.$$

Identity: A clear and simple mark, with concrete and legally defensible attributes. This is how brand originated – from the red-hot iron used to stamp the owners' name on cattle.

Reputation: Psychological benefits resulting from a particular set of associations in the mind of customers. These differentiate it from competitors and create a promise of future performance, which constitutes the reputation of the business.

Brand is a result, an effect of everything else that happens in the business. Brand is created and managed through the customer experience – the points at which the company interacts with customers and potential customers. These points of interaction include traditional marketing activities, including both visual and verbal communications, and all the products and operations of the business.

Brand is different from other assets, in that it acquires a power and existence of its own, that is, it becomes a cause, as well as an effect. Brand establishes a non-rational hold over the buying behavior of the customer. This creates a pact between customer and the company, which guarantees a flow of future sales and profits (see Figure 2.10).

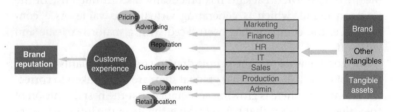

Figure 2.10   Brand as both cause and effect

Thus, from a brand valuation point of view, brand creates value primarily on the demand side of the business, through the impact it has on customer buying decisions. Brand influences two major aspects of the demand chain: sales and margins.

Sales: Brand directly impacts sales in two ways. In the first place, brand influences a prospective customer's decision to buy a product. When faced with a choice between two similar items, the customer is likely to be swayed by each product's image and reputation. This will include such factors as: the name and appearance of the product and packaging (brand identity); communications about the product including both advertising and the opinions and recommendations of other people (reputation). All these things affect the first-time purchaser's view of quality, relevance and desirability. By increasing preference for a company's products or services, brand helps to grow market share. Secondly, as well as influencing the original decision to buy a product or service, brand plays an even more important role in affecting the customer's decision to make repeat purchases of the product and become a loyal customer. It is the power of brand to retain customers which drives the greater proportion of value. As we all know, loyal customers also buy more, and can be persuaded to purchase other products associated with the brand. The bond which brand creates with loyal customers increases the security of future revenue streams. Millward Brown's analysis of 10 years of brand equity data from BrandZ provides evidence that across almost all products and services, bonded customers are the most valuable customers (see Figure 2.11).

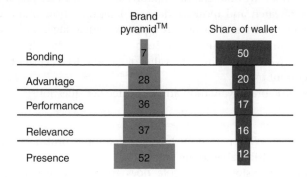

Figure 2.11 Bonded customers are the most valuable customers

Margins: Brand can also have a positive impact on a company's margins, by enabling it to charge higher prices for its products. The price which customers are prepared to pay for a brand often has little to do with the physical qualities of the product or service. Rather, it reflects the meaning which the brand is perceived to add to their lives. Brands command price premiums in many categories – not just luxury goods, but also consumer products, cars, computers and petroleum. Even in categories where it is difficult to obtain a price premium, such as, for example, mobile telephony, brand can have a positive impact on margins. By increasing customer loyalty, brand reduces churn and leads to lower customer acquisition costs. Bonded customers are always the most profitable.

Brand valuation sets out to measure both the incremental sales created by brand (the volume premium) and the additional margins (the price premium). Sometimes both are found together (e.g., with car brands); other brands trade one off against the other. Gucci is a brand that trades off a volume premium for a price premium (selling less at higher prices); Wal-mart is a brand that trades off price premium for a volume premium (selling more at lower prices). There is no right or wrong answer – it is a strategic choice. Either approach can create a valuable brand, if the balance is right.

The preferred approach to brand valuation is the 'Economic Use' method, because, as has been explained above, it is the only approach that can be used to identify the sources of value, and therefore the only one that has both financial and management applications. A robust Economic Use valuation differs from other methods in that it involves not only financial calculations but also the analysis of quantitative research and industry data to determine how brand drives sales and profits and creates competitive advantage. The starting point for any application of the Economic Use method is a baseline valuation which quantifies the value of a brand to its current owner, in its current usage.

A baseline brand valuation answers three key questions:

1. Financial: What part of the business' economic profits on tangible assets is attributable to the brand?
2. Customer Insight: What role does the brand play in driving customer choice?

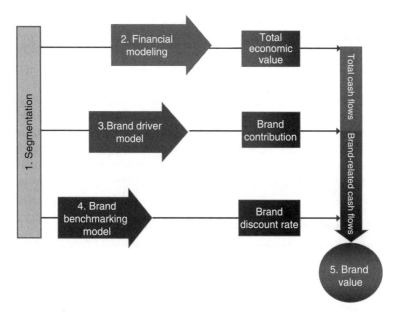

Figure 2.12 Brand valuation methodology – Work steps

3. Strategic: What part of the business' competitive advantage is attributable to the brand?

It does so, in five analytical steps:

1. Segmentation
2. Financial forecasting
3. Brand driver analysis
4. Brand risk analysis
5. Brand value calculation.

These are illustrated in Figure 2.12.

6.1 Brand Valuation Step 1: Segmentation

The first step is to segment the business into relevant components of value. This means identifying the best way to divide up the business from a brand point of view. This is where a brand valuation starts to diverge from the type of business valuation performed by accountants and analysts. Although we call this 'segmentation', this doesn't necessarily imply a pure customer segmentation. The objective is to drill down to the point at which brand behaves differently. Depending on the business, the brand valuation segmentation can include customer segments, products, channels and geography, often a mixture of all of these. The brand is valued separately in each segment, individual segment values are then added up to produce a total value for the brand. This 'bottom up' approach enables us to account for differences in brand strength and importance within different parts of a business, and is essential to provide a robust measurement of brand value.

6.2   Brand Valuation Step 2: Financial Analysis

Once the segments have been agreed upon, historical financial results and financial forecasts are obtained and used to calculate the future cash flows for each segment. In a robust valuation these are derived from internal company P&Ls and strategic plans, which alone allow the necessary level of drill down into segments. Additional analysis may be needed, working with the finance department, to allocate operating profit by brand valuation segment. Apart from the selection of segments, this part of the work is the same as that which would be conducted for a business valuation. From a financial perspective, the correct approach should be to use 'economic profit cash flows', that is free cash flows minus a capital charge to account for the capital employed (the company's cost of capital multiplied by the capital employed). Often, however, a NOPAT number is used instead of free cash flows, and a capital charge is applied to that number to arrive at economic profit. Financial forecasts are generally 3–5 years, after which a terminal value calculation is used. The exception is emerging markets, where it may be necessary to take a longer-term future view.

6.3   Brand Valuation Step 3: Brand Driver Analysis

The next step is to isolate the portion of the cash flows which can be attributed to the brand from overall cash flows. This is the heart of the analysis since it forms the mechanism by which brand value is separated from overall business value. A 'brand driver analysis' is employed to understand the contribution brand makes to driving revenue and profits. The analysis addresses two key questions: 'What are the drivers of the customer purchase decision?' and 'What role does brand play in that decision?' The reasoning is that the customer decision to purchase drives 100 percent of demand (if no money changes hands, there are no cash flows).

In a robust brand valuation, the brand driver analysis is based on statistical analysis of quantitative market research data. Ideally, this is a custom-designed piece of research, tailored for brand valuation purposes. In some cases, it can be possible to re-run existing research data, either brand health and equity studies, such as Millward Brown's Brand Dynamics, and/or customer satisfaction studies, to provide the answers that the brand valuation needs. Depending on the type of business and data availability, statistical techniques used may include multi-variate regression, conjoint analysis and so on. The importance of a quantitative approach to the brand driver analysis cannot be overstated. The application of less robust methods, such as those practiced by Interbrand and Brand Finance, and generally based on estimation, limits the output to a brand valuation number. A quantitative brand driver analysis makes it possible not only to determine the overall role of brand in driving customer decision making, but to identify the effectiveness of brand at each touch point of the customer experience. With this level of granularity, results become actionable for brand strategy and marketing investment decision-making.

A robust brand driver analysis has two outputs: a determination of what portion of future cash flows can reasonably be attributed to the impact of brand, as opposed to everything else that happens in the business (product, pricing, distribution, customer service and so forth); and identification of the sources of brand value by customer experience touch point. Especially when brand driver analysis is conducted for the brand and its competitors, it becomes possible to measure brand strength and effectiveness and gaps by touch point.

6.4   Brand Valuation Step 4: Competitor Brand Benchmarking

In accordance with standard valuation principles, the portion of cash flows that the brand driver analysis identifies as created by brand for each segment has to be discounted to obtain a net present value for the brand. In a business valuation, the discount rate is calculated from the company's WACC (weighted average cost of capital), together with, when appropriate, additional factors relating to industry and country risk. In a brand valuation, the discount rate applied to the portion of future cash flows identified as created by brand includes an additional factor, which takes into account the specific risks associated with the brand.

The concept is that brand may be more or less risky than the business as a whole. Generally brand carries more risk. Brand is reputation and as such can be easily damaged: by both major events such as accounting scandals and operational incidents and more incremental factors such as a decline in customer service or product quality. However, there are instances where brand carries less risk than the business. The old AT&T in long-distance fixed-line telephony is a good example. AT&T had a great brand, on a business which had little or no future. The lower risk of the brand was demonstrated by the fact that when you took the good brand off the bad business, and put it onto a better business, such as wireless, it had the power to drive significant additional revenues and profits.

There are various alternative ways of calculating the brand risk factor. The most robust of these is through a quantitative measurement of brand strength or risk relative to competitors (from a brand management standpoint, the measurement is strength; from a financial viewpoint, the concept is turned upside down and becomes risk). In Millward Brown Optimor's brand valuation model, depicted above, a Brand Benchmarking model is used to determine the security and stability of brand-related cash flows. This is an Excel-based model of brand strength on ten key metrics, relating to brand presence and brand quality. These are quantitatively derived from industry metrics, such as market share, growth rates and research metrics, such as brand awareness, consideration and so on. Metrics are recalculated as a linear function on a scale of 1–10. The total index score is used to calculate a brand discount rate, which is applied to the business discount rate. One of the advantages of this approach is that in addition to a brand discount rate, it produces strategic insights into brand strengths and weaknesses, and KPIs to use in measuring progress.

6.5   Brand Valuation Step 5: Brand Value Calculation

In the final step, the brand contribution percentage from the brand driver analysis is applied to the financial cash flows of each segment to calculate the portion of those cash flows attributable to brand. The

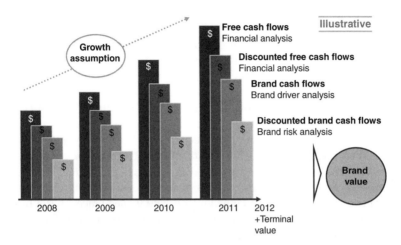

Figure 2.13 Illustration of brand value calculation

brand-related cash flows are then discounted at the brand risk rate derived as a function of the brand strength score and the business risk (weighted average cost of capital, etc.). The output is a brand value for each segment. The total value of the brand is the sum of the value in each segment (see Figure 2.13).

7 Applications of brand valuation

Brand valuation is, in its essence, a method for linking brand to financial performance. This makes it extremely flexible in its application. It is an approach which can be used to address many different needs and questions which arise in a business about the value of brand and marketing. Applications can be divided into three main groups – financial, strategic and measurement/management.

7.1 Financial applications of brand valuation

The major 'Financial' applications of brand valuation include balance sheet reporting and compliance, M&A and IPOs, licensing and royalty rate determination, securitization, litigation support and investor relations.

7.1.1 *Balance sheet reporting and compliance*

The bulk of brand valuations conducted by accounting firms relate to balance sheet reporting to comply with IFRS 3 and FAS 141 and 142, whose requirements were explained earlier in this chapter. This divides into: an initial valuation of brands on acquisition; annual revaluation to test whether the brand value on the balance sheet has been 'impaired', that is, has declined in value. Almost all major corporations in the consumer packaged goods and luxury industries in Europe and many of those in the United States now recognize brands on their balance sheets and go through the annual testing process. So, for example, in 2008, Christian Dior/LVMH placed a value of €10.3 billion on Louis Vuitton, PPR valued Gucci at around the same amount. Other companies putting large brand values on their balance sheets include Pernod Ricard (€7.7 billion), Cadbury Schweppes (€4 billion) and Unilever (€3.9 billion). These brand values are dwarfed by Procter & Gamble, which carries $30 billion of brand value on its balance sheet. The majority of this is for the Gillette brand, which was acquired in 2005, just after the new rules had come into effect.

7.1.2 *Mergers & Acquisitions and IPOs*

Brand valuations are increasingly being conducted as part of M&A and IPO transactions. In an M&A situation, brand valuation may be initiated by the buyer or the seller. Occasionally, the two sides will agree to have a joint brand valuation conducted by an independent third party. For the seller, the attraction of brand valuation is obvious: to make sure that the value of the brand is fully reflected in the price paid for the business, and increase the amount of money he gets for the deal. For the buyer, brand valuation can help to determine if he is paying too much or too little, if he is getting a bargain, or if he is being taken advantage of.

There are two aspects of brand value which should be considered in brand valuation for deal purposes: the current value of the brand and the potential or option value of the brand. The current value represents the value the brand contributes to the business that is being sold, that is, its intrinsic value to the seller, as part of his business assets. The potential or option value represents the new value that the purchased brand will add to the buyer's existing businesses.

Depending on the situation, acquiring a brand may add a great deal of value to the buyer's business.

An example is the sale of the John Hancock insurance and asset management business. John Hancock's CEO, David D'Alessandro, a marketer with a sophisticated appreciation of brand, commissioned a valuation of the John Hancock brand, which was carried out by current members of the Millward Brown Optimor team. He used the results to negotiate a significant price premium in the business in 2003 to Manu Life, a Canadian insurer, which lacked a strong brand in the United States.

Brand valuation is also increasingly undertaken as part of the planning for IPOs. Brand valuation provides an important communication tool to the investment community, helping to ensure that full value of the businesses assets is reflected in the offering price. It can also have a major impact on deal structure. For example, Brand valuation conducted by Millward Brown Optimor played an important part in determining the way which Visa went public in March 2008. At an initial offering price of $17.9 billion, Visa's IPO was the largest in history.

7.1.3 Licensing and royalty rate determination

A growing number of corporations are now using brand valuation as a tool for determining royalty rates. Best practices Economic Use brand valuation techniques are ideally suited to this. The approach is to identify the additional revenues and profits which can be generated for the licensee by using the licensor's more powerful brand on their products and services. This is done by conducting market research to compare the effectiveness of the licensor vs. the licensee brand in driving purchase behavior. This information is then fed into a brand valuation model, to determine the sales and profit uplift, which is then used to calculate equivalent royalty rates. The result is a royalty rate which bears a direct relationship to the value that the licensed brand generated – a much sounder foundation for negotiations. In situations such as internal licensing for large global conglomerates, when it would be impractical to do a full brand valuation among B2B customers, a modified approach is used. This applies an index, based on brand strength measures, to vary a standard rate which is derived from comparables.

7.1.4   Other financial applications

There are a number of additional uses of brand valuation for financial purposes, which are less frequently observed. These include: securitization of brands, litigation support and investor relations.

In brand securitization, brands are valued and used as assets to back specific lines of credit. In many cases, the securitization has been initiated by media companies and is related to the valuing of future royalty rate streams from brand licenses. For example, Disney has issued bonds to monetize expected royalties from licensing the right to use Mickey Mouse and its other brands to Oriental Land Company, which owns and operates the Tokyo Disneyworld. Other examples of securitization have often involved media and music rights.

Brand valuation is regularly used in litigation support. Typical examples include: law suits against trademark infringement (Gucci has successfully pursued illegal users of its brand), and cases brought by the IRS against companies suspected of evading taxes through brand licensing (e.g., against DHL).

Brand valuation numbers can prove very useful in communicating to the financial community. Corporations often reference the value of their brands in annual reports to persuade investors value of these brands justifies an increase in share price. Vodafone is a case in point.

7.2   Strategic Applications of Brand Valuation

Financial applications of brand valuation are intrinsically less interesting than strategic and brand management applications. Financial applications are about extracting greater financial advantage out of current brand value; strategic and brand management applications seek to make the future pie bigger, that is, to leverage brand better to grow the value which it adds to the corporation.

Brand valuation can be applied to almost any aspect of brand strategy. Three of the most common applications are discussed here: brand strategy development, brand architecture and brand growth strategy.

7.2.1   Brand strategy development

Before making any major decisions about brand strategy, it is customary and only common sense, to conduct an initial brand audit, or assessment of the current state of the brand. This enables the company to understand the brand's strengths, weaknesses and leverage points, in the context of competitors' strategy, the brand's current and potential customers and the evolving future marketplace. Although a lot of good work is done, brand assessment is traditionally conducted in a rather unsystematic fashion. The inputs include qualitative management and customer interviews, a review of existing research data, and, in the best cases, some new quantitative market research. There is no framework for evaluating the brand – the information is compiled and conclusions made in a subjective fashion. This places over much reliance on the brand consultant or brand manager's judgment and expertise.

Emerging best practices includes not only a qualitative assessment of brand perceptions but also a quantitative analysis of brand performance. The inputs include not only qualitative and quantitative research on the brand, but in addition, a brand valuation is conducted to link the brand assessment to company financial performance.

The advantage of this approach is that it allows the state of the brand to be measured on hard financial as well as softer metrics. Most importantly, it sets up a model of how brand creates value in the business. This becomes the foundation for brand strategy development. It both provides a framework for idea generation, and a dynamic model which can be used to test the financial impact of alternative brand strategy and positioning options.

7.2.2 Brand architecture

Brand architecture is one of the most powerful applications of the brand valuation model. Decisions about brand architecture and brand naming can have major business consequences. Brand architecture impacts marketing investment levels and effectiveness, the clarity and impact of the offering; and, above all, customer loyalty and purchase behavior. The wrong brand architecture decision can lead to significant customer loss and decline in market share.

Especially in the aftermath of an acquisition, brand architecture decisions are difficult to make. The issues are emotional and political. The CEO of the acquired brand will almost always claim that changing the name will lead to loss of sales. Sometimes this is very true, sometimes not true at all, and, most often, partly true.

Brand valuation can help to raise the debate to a more objective level, by putting facts and figures around brand architecture issues.

The first step is to conduct an Economic Use valuation of the brands in question. This establishes the current strength and effectiveness of each brand. Alternative brand architecture scenarios can then be developed and run through the brand valuation model. The objective is to identify the solution which will generate most future revenues, profits and value for the business, taking into account the different levels of investment that each option will require.

AT&T is an example of a company that has used brand valuation analysis as a key input to decision-making about brand architecture. Data about the value and strength of the AT&T brand, conducted by Millward Brown Optimor, led its acquirer, SBC, to take the counter-intuitive decision and rebrand all its businesses, including SBC, Bell South and Cingular, to AT&T. The new AT&T is today the most valuable and fastest growing telecommunications brand in the United States.

7.2.3   Brand Growth Strategy

Brand valuation can not only be used to assist in decision-making about existing businesses; it can also be applied to identify, plan and implement opportunities to extend a brand into new businesses and markets, in a way that maximizes chances of success and minimizes risk. This analysis seeks to leverage the unique transferable nature of the brand asset, the fact that, unlike other assets, brand can be separated from the business in which it originates and transplanted to new areas, to generate additional revenues and profits. This application of brand valuation is in high demand during times of economic downturn, when companies' attention is focused on extracting as much value as possible from existing assets. The brand provides a means of entering new areas of opportunity, and generating new revenue streams without having to spend on acquisitions.

In this case, the brand valuation is focused not on how the brand generates value in its current applications, but on the potential for the brand to create additional value in new applications. The analysis starts by developing a thorough understanding of how the brand creates value in its existing uses. The focus then turns to assessing the brand's chances of success in new areas, through industry analysis, market sizing and competitor analysis, qualitative and quantitative research into purchase behavior and brand fit with the new categories. The final output is selection of the opportunities where the brand has the potential to add the most value and development of a business plan on how exactly to enter the new categories. Very often, the entry strategy includes licensing the brand to third parties. This is the lowest risk way of entering a new category – get someone else to make the investment, and just take back a risk-free stream of royalties from the brand.

Companies which have recently used this approach to generate new revenue streams from their brands span a wide range of industries – from hospitality and retail, to computer hardware, to media.

7.3 Brand management/measurement applications of brand valuation

Best practices in brand management imply the introduction of the same level of accountability in management of the brand asset, as is required in the management of other business assets. This means that the level and allocation of investment in the brand should be determined based on a robust assessment of the expected financial returns. Then, after the fact, the actual results should be measured, and the learnings applied to optimize the next year's budget. In other words, ROI measurement and investment optimization.

To meet these goals requires the ability to link the impact of different types of marketing investment to financial value creation. In the context of IMC, this presents particular challenges.

The development of a successful IMC strategy demands knowledge and understanding on the part of the marketer of how each individual marketing initiative impacts the target audience. Increasingly this means not only on-line and off-line advertising and promotions, but also sponsorship, events, PR, social marketing and product placement. Strategy development is dependent on the availability of data which can be used to predict the effects of each initiative. Only then is it possible to determine each initiative's appropriate place in the mix and the amount of budget to be allocated to it.

Demonstrating the success of integrated marketing presents even greater difficulties. For the results of an integrated marketing campaign to be measured, an integrated methodology for measurement is required. Current forms of measurement are evolving rapidly to meet the needs of the IMC environment. A variety of communications measurements and optimization tools are available to the marketing professional, ranging from the tried and true to the newly developed and experimental. However, closer examination of these tools reveals how challenging it is to apply them in a holistic fashion. Each has its own function and purpose, addressing one particular aspect of measurement. As each operates separately from the others, there is no consistent answer – rather a series of answers, each tackling part of the question.

Figure 2.14 is a disguised example from a real client (a major global brand) and illustrates the dilemma. Current tools operate at different Altitudes: from the big picture (Market Mix Modeling and Brand Equity Tracking) to a great degree of granularity (e.g., campaign-specific copy testing or impressions-based analysis). They address different questions – From: How well are my brands doing at converting up the loyalty pyramid? To: What was the impact of a particular campaign? They use different types of Metrics to measure results: Consumer perceptions; Awareness; Impressions; Incremental sales per £ spent. They measure at different frequencies and in different places: from continuous and global, to selective and limited, to experiments in individual markets.

There is an obvious need to take measurement to the next level and develop a holistic approach which can be used to measure the results of past campaigns and enhance future communications effectiveness. The demand is for an approach which will enable companies to come

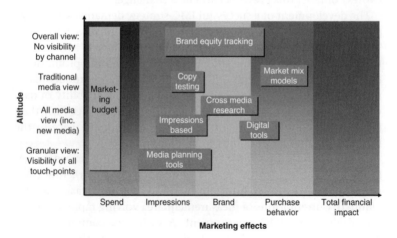

Figure 2.14 Fragmentation of marketing measurements

to a single decision about how the organization should allocate its marketing money most effectively. This will then make it possible to optimize the total return from IMC investments against strategic goals.

A way has to be found to integrate the different tools, bring them all down to the same level, and create a common currency for measurement. In the end, there is very little argument and, frankly, no choice as to what this common currency has to be. Money is the common metric in use across organizations. Financial results are the test by which all endeavors are, in the final result, judged. Brand valuation tools and techniques are ideally suited to fulfill this integrating function, forming the means by which different metrics and measures can be linked to money.

A holistic marketing ROI and optimization model has to integrate four discrete measurements:

1. The direct impact of marketing on sales
2. The indirect impact of marketing on brand (long term and short term)
3. The impact of brand on sales
4. Financial value created and ROI.

This is illustrated in Figure 2.15.

Each of these measurements is currently conducted in isolation from the others, involving one or more discrete analytical processes.

7.3.1 Measuring the direct impact of marketing on sales – Sales Response Modeling

The standard way of measuring investment in brand and marketing is 'sales response' or 'marketing mix' modeling. These models

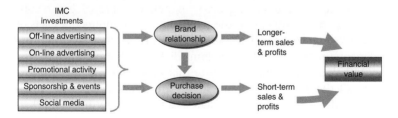

Figure 2.15 Total marketing ROI model concept

use econometrics, which are complicated to implement, but founded on a simple idea: correlate past spend on different marketing activities against the sales that resulted. The most sophisticated of these, described by my colleague Peter Cain in another chapter, produce a very granular and valuable picture of the direct sales impact of traditional marketing investments, particularly advertising. There is nothing else available that provides such detail on what happened when we spent a dollar on TV versus a dollar on print or on-line advertising and whatever other relevant items data is available for.

Even the best of these models have some serious limitations. The most important of these are:

- No real link to financials. ROI is defined as incremental sales generated by marketing measured against the marketing investment put in by the company. Sales are measured in retail prices, not the much lower wholesale price which the company is paid. This is obviously misleading, an imaginary number which has no relationship to actual financial results, and does not link into the strategic planning and value creation models most companies use for budgeting.
- A short-term orientation. The best sales response models do a good job of answering the question they ask, which is: 'if we spent a dollar on TV versus Promotions or Print over the last 2–3 years, what immediate uplift on sales did we get?' Results naturally skew in favor of promotional activities which are designed to provide a short-term increase in sales and discriminate against advertising, much of which is directed to building brand longer term.
- No measurement of brand effects. Sales response modeling measures the direct impact of marketing investments on sales only. It ignores the fact that the same dollar also has an indirect effect on sales, through its impact on consumer perceptions of the brand. Marketing investment impacts sales indirectly through brand both in the short term and in the longer term. The indirect impacts of marketing on financial results are at least as great as and often many times greater than the immediate direct impacts.
- A third issue is that marketing mix modeling has only limited predictive capabilities. Simulations and market allocation models only work for the immediate future, assuming no changes in market conditions.

Over use of sales response models can lead companies down dangerous paths of over-promoting, to a degree which can do serious damage to their brand. General Motors is a famous example. In an attempt to boost sales, the company at one point offered an employee discount to everyone. Not surprisingly it worked – sales did go up. The sales response models unfortunately were unable to measure the negative impact that these promotions had on perceptions of car quality, which ultimately did far more damage to the brand and the business than was offset by the temporary lift in sales.

7.3.2 *Measuring the indirect impact of marketing on brand – Cross Media*

The second piece of the puzzle is therefore to devise a method to measure the impact of marketing activities on brand. Until recently, approaches to this have suffered from some serious limitations. The most important of these are: they have been partial in their design; they have been based on inaccurate estimates of exposure to different activities; and, above all, it has been almost impossible to parse out the impacts of different elements of the marketing mix.

The most common variants are traditional advertising tracking designs as well as a range of exposed/unexposed comparative research designs. These designs have been suitable for understanding the overall contribution of the largely TV-focused brand campaigns of yesteryear. But they are not generally capable of picking up the individual impacts of the multiplicity of activities used in a modern communications campaign, such as on-line advertising, search, product placement and events as well as a wider range of traditional media.

Considerable progress has been made over the last few years in developing a more 'econometric' approach to measuring the brand impacts of marketing. As described by Peter Cain in his chapter on the subject, these apply mix modeling techniques to brand metrics. Time-series brand tracking data is incorporated into sales response models, which are allowed to evolve over time, providing a longer-term and more accurate picture of brand impacts on sales.

But even these more 'econometric' solutions to measuring marketing impacts fall down when it comes to identifying the contributions made to brand building by the ever more complicated array of communications involved in today's integrated marketing campaigns.

Some of the more effective solutions are those which don't try to capture the full effects of IMC, instead concentrating on the brand impacts of one particular strand of marketing activity. A simple, yet very effective approach has been developed for sponsorship measurement. This uses the brand valuation and brand driver models as the base case. Research is then conducted to measure change in attitudes to the brand among people aware of and interested in the company's sponsorship of a particular event. Changes in brand perceptions are then fed through the brand driver model, the uplifts captured and translated into incremental sales. This approach has been applied successfully to measuring the ROI from major sponsorship investments. Visa, for example, uses its brand valuation model to measure the ROI from its sponsorship of the Olympic Games. It solves a major problem with sponsorship measurement, which is that the major impact tends to be on brand, and therefore is not captured by marketing mix modeling. It only works, however, when the investment and its impact are big enough and limited enough in duration, for the split between before and after to be easily demarcated.

The approach which comes closest to fully measuring the effects of an integrated marketing campaign is CrossMedia Modeling. This originated in work conducted by Dynamic Logic, the Internet advertising research unit within Millward Brown. The Millward Brown researchers were struggling to find a reliable way of measuring the brand impact of on-line marketing investments, which didn't show up properly either in traditional mix modeling or in traditional advertising tracking research. The solution lies in devising a sound answer to the problem of the complex overlapping patterns of reach and frequency of exposure in multimedia campaigns. Many new digital media, as well as some more targeted traditional media, go deeper in their impact on the audiences they reach, but reach much narrower audiences than say TV.

The first and simplest research methodologies tested reactions among samples of people aware of the different campaigns elements and compared these to unaware samples – the same principle used in sponsorship ROI measurement. The problem with these approaches is that it is often hard to identify appropriate samples, due to low reach and misattribution of recall between the various media activities, which are typically using very similar creative in integrated campaigns. Furthermore comparisons were often distorted by the underlying differences in the pre-existing brand relationships of the different media audiences, especially between more broadcast media such as TV and more narrowly targeted, focused activities like many of the new digital opportunities.

The latest approach takes many of these issues off the table by avoiding the use of conscious awareness or recall measures altogether. Instead, respondent samples are classified based on their probable weight of exposure to each of the different media elements in a campaign. Then multivariate modeling techniques are used to parse out the effects of exposure to the different campaign elements on key brand measures.

The robustness of the research derives from two key elements. Firstly, the analysis is founded on an empirical data of the relevant media behaviors of the respondents – what magazines they read, when and how much they view TV, what websites they are exposed to and what their patterns of travel are for out of home exposures. This data is captured in the same survey that captures data on respondents brand perceptions and is combined with other sources such as cookies identifying exposure to on-line activities as well as calibrated against media company data on campaign delivery, and so on. Secondly the design builds in controls for the variations in underlying, pre-existing brand relationships across the different media audiences reached by the campaign, which otherwise can confound the precision of the reads on the contributions of activities in those media.

The result is a more accurate reading of the brand impacts of both the traditional and non-traditional elements of a campaign, in one single piece of research. The data on the brand impacts of each type of media provide the basis for a more accurate analysis of ROI by IMC activity, and a more powerful optimization tool.

7.33 & 7.3.4   Measuring the impact of brand on sales and linking to financial value creation – Brand valuation

Two additional steps are required to complete the picture.

The first is to fill in the missing link between brand and sales. Brand valuation offers a way to do this. As has been described, the Brand Driver analysis measures the impact of brand on customer buying behavior and, through this, on sales. This brand impact consists of the built-up equity from past marketing activities as well as the other touch points of the customer experience. In this way, it lays down the base case for brand impact on sales, against which the specific impacts of individual marketing activities can be measured.

The second step is to link the direct and indirect sales impact of modeling to business financials to measure value creation and ROI. Again, the brand valuation model provides the means to do this. The data on both the direct and indirect impacts of each type of media can be fed into the brand valuation model. Other types of marketing measurement, such as quality of advertising (from copy testing) and perceptions of innovation quality, can be incorporated at a higher level of analysis, to complete the picture, and ensure that all relevant factors are considered in evaluation of marketing effectiveness. The outputs are: a robust reading on marketing ROI by activity; and a dynamic model of how marketing strategy and investment impact financial results, short and longer term, which can be used for marketing budget optimization and financial planning. The valuation model thus becomes the true integrator, used to convert all metrics into the only common currency for measurement – money.

8   Summary and conclusions

Brand valuation is about more than just a number. When combined with robust market research and industry data, it becomes an important management tool. Demand for brand valuation has risen over the past 20 years, as a result of the growth in intangible assets as a proportion of shareholder value. Originating as a form of acquisition accounting, it has evolved into a means of measuring and managing the impact of brand and marketing on business performance. There are a number of different types of brand valuation methodologies. These can be divided into external, market-based approaches, which just provide a number; incomplete approaches, which look at only one aspect of brand value; and internal or 'Economic Use' brand valuations. The latter is the preferred approach, since it is the only one which provides both a robust financial value for the brand and insight into how brand value is created. Rules and standards for brand valuation have emerged, as accounting, tax and operational standards bodies have started to recognize the large amount of value at stake. While they represent a step in the right direction, some of these standards are highly illogical, others vague. The accounting standards only allow acquired brands to be put on the balance sheet, not brands such as Coca Cola which have been created internally. Tax authorities treat brands as a transfer pricing issue. The ISO standard, due out in 2010, is all-inclusive and approves dubious forms of valuation such as cost-based approaches, which assume that the value of a brand is equal to the money spent to create it. Best practices in brand valuation starts from the premise that, the most accurate way to quantify the value that brand adds to a business is to take a 'bottom up' approach, which measures the sources of brand value. The focus is on quantifying the impact of the brand on the demand side of the business, through a calculation of the 'volume premium' and the 'value premium' attributable to brand. The methodology involves not only financial models, but also market research analysis to identify the drivers of the customer purchase decision, and the impact of brand on that decision. A baseline brand valuation quantifies the value of the brand to the current owner, in the current business. It includes five analytical steps: segmentation, financial forecasting, brand driver analysis, brand risk analysis and brand value calculation. The baseline brand valuation not only provides a value for the brand; it sets up a model of how brand creates value in the business. This can then be used dynamically, as a scenario planning tool, to calculate the financial impact of alternative brand strategy and marketing investment options. Brand valuation is essentially a method for linking brand to financial performance. It is very flexible and has many different applications. These can be divided into three main groups – financial, strategic and measurement/management. Financial applications of brand valuation include: balance sheet reporting and compliance; M&A and IPOs; licensing and royalty rate determination; investor relations and securitization. The most common strategic applications of brand valuation are: brand strategy development; resolving brand architecture issues; and identifying the best brand growth strategies. Brand valuation can also be used to implement best practices in brand management and measurement, introducing true accountability into the marketing function. The growth of integrated marketing campaigns presents new challenges. Developing an IMC strategy requires data which predicts the effects of each initiative. Demonstrating the success of IMC necessitates an integrated methodology for measurement. Current measurement tools are as fragmented as the initiatives themselves, and operate at different 'altitudes'. Brand valuation can be used as the integrator, linking other forms of measurement, by bringing them down to the only common currency for measurement – money. A holistic marketing ROI and optimization model combines four discrete measurements: the direct impact of marketing on sales, the indirect impact of marketing on brand (long term and short term); the impact of brand on sales; financial value created and ROI. The direct impact of marketing on sales can be obtained from traditional marketing mix models. New 'Cross Media' techniques can be used to compare the brand impacts of both the non-traditional and traditional elements of a campaign, on an equal footing. Brand valuation provides the two missing pieces – the link between brand and sales, and the link to financial value creation. The power of brand valuation lies in its simplicity and credibility, its integration capabilities and its flexibility as a financial, strategic and management tool. Brand valuation puts marketing on an equal footing with other types of investment made by the company, elevating its position and stature. Brand value is the ultimate marketing metric and one everyone should be using.

References

Abdallah, Wagdy M. and Murtuza, Athar, 'Transfer Pricing Strategies of Intangible Assets, E-Commerce and International Taxation of Multinationals', *International Tax Journal*, 2006, Vol. 15, Spring, 5–17.

Beruch, Lev, *Intangibles: Measurement, Management & Reporting*, Brookings Institution Press: Washington DC, 2001.

Die Tank AG, 'Imarken Bewertung', Absatzwirtschaft, 2004.

Ernst & Young, 'Consumer Products IFRS Financial Statements Survey', November 2008.

Financial Accounting Standards Board (FASB), 'Goodwill and Other Intangible Assets', Statement of Financial Accounting Standards No. 142, as amended 2008, www.fasb.org/st/summary/stsum142.shtml, accessed 1 January 2010.

Gerzema, John and Lebar, Ed., *The Brand Bubble*, Wiley & Sons: San Francisco, 2008.

'Global Brands', *Financial Times*, 29 April 2009 (Source: Millward Brown Optimor – including data from BrandZ, Datamonitor and Bloomberg).

Haxthausen, Ove, 'Valuing Brands and Brand Investments: Key Learnings and Future Expectations', *Journal of Brand Management*, 2009, Vol. 17, I, 18–25.

Hollis, Nigel, *The Global Brand*, Palgrave MacMillan: Basingstoke, UK, 2008.

International Accounting Standards Board, 'Summary of IFRS 3', iasplus.com/standard/ifrs03.htm, accessed 15 December 2009.

International Organization for Standards (ISO), 'POC 231. Brand Valuation, Working Draft', September 1009.

IRS, 'Regulations Outlining Transfer Pricing', 26 CFR 1.482, 4 January 2004.

Lindeman, Jan, 'Brand Valuation: The Financial Value of Brands', The BrandChannel.com, 27 April 2004, http://www.brandchannel.com/images/papers/future%20of%20brands.pdf, accessed 6 April 2010.

Millward, Brown, 'What Matters? Winning Strategies for Ad Agencies', *American Advertising Agency Association (AAAA)*, April 2007.

Millward, Brown Optimor, 'The BrandZ Top 100 Most Valuable Global Brands', 2009, https://www.millwardbrown.com/Sites/Optimor/Content/KnowledgeCenter/BrandzRanking.aspx, accessed 6 April 2010.

Moore, Lindsay Dr., 'Brand Valuation Basics', KLM Inc., 2002, http://www.klminc.com/brand_valuation/bvbasics.html, accessed 6 April 2010.

OECD Model Tax Convention, 'Tax Guidelines on Transfer Pricing', 1995, updated version 2001.

Official Journal of the European Union, 'Resolution of the Council and of the Representatives of the Governments of the Member States on a Code of Conduct on Transfer Pricing Documentation for Associated Enterprises in the European Union (EU TPD)', 27 June 2006.

Schmitt, Bernd H. and Rogers, David L., *Handbook on Brand and Experience Management*, Edward Elgar Publishing: Cheltenham, 2008.

Seddon, Joanna, 'Firms that Build Brand Value Will Be Recession Survivors', *Admap*, May 2009.

The Ministry of Economy, Trade and Industry, the Government of Japan, 'The Report of the Committee on Brand Valuation', 24 June 2002.

United Nations, 'Seminar on Addressing Information Gaps in Business and Macro-Economic Accounts to Better Explain Economic Performance; Guidelines on Brand Valuation', New York, June 2006.

Mard, Michael J., Hitchner, James R. and Hyden, Steven D., *Valuation for Financial Reporting: Value Measurements and Reporting, Intangible Assets, Goodwill and Impairment*, Second edition, John Wiley & Sons inc.: London, 2007.

Tollington, Tony, *Brand Assets*, Wiley & Sons: London, 2002.

Wan, Lixin, 'Branding: The Next Step', *China International Business*, February 2006.

3
Marketing Communication Measurement in a Transformational Marketplace

Don E. Schultz

This chapter illustrates a process for measuring the returns on brand marketing activities in what is termed a 'transformational marketplace'. Simply put, the argument is that brand marketing and marketing communication are being transformed by a number of internal and external factors. All will radically change how the discipline will operate now, develop in the future and be practiced and measured going forward. Figure 3.1 illustrates the general discontinuity brand marketing and communication are undergoing.

Recent changes and events in globalization, marketplace development, consumers, technology and communication systems make it almost impossible to continue the brand marketing and communication practices developed over the last half-century. Where, in the past, marketers, their agencies and the media systems could generally identify the various changes which were occurring, and, from that, adapt and adjust their business processes to meet those identifiable challenges, today, the cataclysmic events, which have come as the result of the explosion of digital technology, global interlocking business practices and the recent economic crisis, have made it next to impossible to evolve the current models to meet the changes required.

Yet, it is still within the framework of this radically changed and changing marketplace that marketing and communication managers must operate and compete. The system is fairly simple: identify the availability of finite organizational resources, then, allocate those resources into brand marketing and communication programs and,

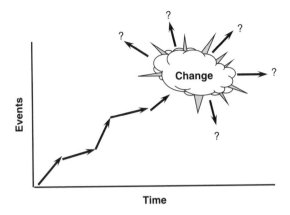

Figure 3.1 Discontinuous change results in marketplace transformations

finally, identify and measure the results, commonly the returns achieved on those investments. The process is certainly not new, but the methods employed demand change. That is the focus of this chapter.

A quick review is first provided to explain what created the current state of brand marketing and communication. The transition from a 'push communication' system to one driven by consumers, that is, a 'push and pull marketplace', comes first. That leads to the need for movement from brand marketing message distribution to consumer brand media and marketing consumption, that is, how consumers take in, process and use the brand marketing activities they choose to access and acquire from marketing organizations. The four key elements in brand media consumption are then identified and suggestions made as to how those might be used to improve brand marketing and communication allocation and measurement today and tomorrow. The chapter ends with a look at what this changed system means for brand marketing organizations and their managers over the next decade.

1   Historical brand communication measurement systems

Traditional brand marketing and communication approaches were developed and codified in the middle-to-latter half of the twentieth century. Such currently revered marketing practices as the 4Ps (1957), the Hierarchy of Effects (1961), media optimization models based on a frequency of three exposures (1965), market/product positioning (1972), market segmentation (1980) and a host of other mass-media-related general marketing and communication concepts were developed during that time. Many of these concepts still underlie the majority of all brand marketing and communication approaches being used today. Even the Unique Selling Proposition (1961) and the ubiquitous 'Big Idea' (mid-1970s) all are firmly rooted in mass market, mass communication approaches developed primarily in the United States and the United Kingdom.

Many brand marketing and communication conventions have been based on Western social norms which have evolved from behaviorist psychological, stimulus-response models developed more than a century ago. Those evolved into the Hierarchy of Effects models (Colley, 1961; Lavidge and Steiner, 1961) which posited the marketer controlled the entire marketing system – the marketer determined the products to be produced, the prices to be asked, the distribution systems to be used and the messages and incentives to be sent out through the various available media forms to persuade customers to buy what the firm had made. That reflected the mantra of the 4Ps and continues to dominate marketing thought even today.

In this marketer controlled system, consumers were considered to be malleable pawns which marketers could influence and persuade, if the right message were used with the right audience at the right time. Brand marketing and communication managers envisioned their activities as the basis for a 'silver bullet' system with near-magical properties that, if properly delivered, would generate wealth for the marketer and happiness for the consumer.

The system, as developed and practiced by most marketers, agencies and even the media organizations who delivered the market-influencing messaging looked something like the illustration in Figure 3.2.

This approach, which was derived from the early studies of mass communication in the 1930s, illustrates how the marketer controls all the variables from product development to consumer communication. A host of internal/external suppliers assist the brand marketer in the development and delivery of the marketing and communication programs. All efforts are directed to previously identified 'target

Figure 3.2 Outbound push marketing system

markets' thought to be prospects for the promoted product or service. The system itself is all outbound and linear, with limited opportunities for consumer feedback. It is always defined by and driven by the marketer.

In spite of all the marketplace changes, this same model has been in use since the 1950s. Developed for Western markets by large-scale consumer product organizations, it has been exported to and imposed on other markets around the world. Brand or marketing communication measurement has generally been after-the-fact, that is, consumer surveys of message or brand recognition and/or recall based on tenuous connections between advertising exposure and consumer attitudinal measures.

The mid-1990s introduction of the Internet and other digital, interactive systems in the West began to drive systemic change. Those are reviewed in the next section.

2 Transitioning to interactive communication systems

The rapid development of the Internet, World Wide Web and ancillary digitally driven communication systems, for example, mobile, social networks and the like, require a major re-thinking of brand marketing and communication. These interactive facilities have radically changed how marketers operate today and how they must operate in the future.

To be clear, the introduction of online media communication has not destroyed the older, outbound-only systems. They have simply been added to the consumer's repertoire of media alternatives. Not everyone stopped reading newspapers when Internet news became available, but sufficient numbers did shift so that the old advertising mass media models have been negatively impacted. Not everyone

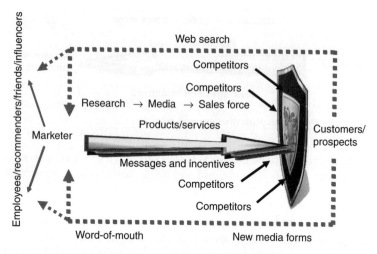

Figure 3.3   Consumer-driven 'push and pull' marketplace

has switched from television to mobile to view entertainment, but in certain parts of the world, sufficient numbers have switched so that the previous efficiencies of traditional mass media have been substantially impacted. It is this transformation, from an outbound only model of brand marketing and communication to one that recognizes and embraces both outbound messaging by the marketer along with inbound access of brand product and communication information by the consumer, is what has created what we now call the 'push-pull marketplace'. That's shown in Figure 3.3.

Marketers, as they have done for the past half-century, continue to 'push' brand messages and incentives out toward customers and prospects, using traditional methods such as advertising, direct marketing, sales promotion, public relations, events and the like. At the same time, consumers have developed a plethora of alternatives to block and avoid those 'pushed out' messages such as remote controls, spam blockers and TiVo. Consumers are primarily seeking to control the marketer's access to them and their lives.

Thus, the outbound brand marketing systems have become increasingly cluttered as marketers attempt to (a) develop new outbound processes and systems that will either pierce the consumer-erected shields, or (b) will be so unique or contain such interesting messages and incentives that consumers will either accept them or access them on their own.

While the marketer continues to send out barrages of brand messages and incentives, the consumer is using the new media forms to access the information they perceive is most important to them. Today, there are a multitude of these new consumer-activated media forms, chief of which are web search, mobile, QSR, downloadable promotional systems and the present-day darlings of social media, that is, MySpace, FaceBook and Twitter. All interactive, that is, they allow consumers to talk with each other, compare notes or experiences about brands, products and services or most distressing to brand marketers, to make fun or ridicule the brand's marketing efforts, as is increasingly occurring.

These new media forms are consumer accessed and consumer controlled, and ones over which marketers have little or no control. The end result is, the consumer not only controls what messages and incentives reach him or her via traditional channels, they also access the media forms they prefer when they need them. This is a dramatic change in the way brand marketing and communication have traditionally been developed and used.

It is this new 'push and pull marketplace' with which all brand managers are struggling, and few have found solutions.

The most important factor is that the critical variables are not what the brand marketer decides to distribute. Instead, it is what the consumer takes in and processes. Where once traditional media almost guaranteed large-scale audiences because of the content they contained, today those audiences have fragmented into hundreds of smaller audiences with more specialized interests and concerns. Thus, the challenge of the brand marketer is not to identify which media forms are most efficient for brand message delivery, but which media forms are accessed by consumers. That means, which media most effectively communicates with consumers. The brand marketing and communication model has clearly shifted from message distribution to message consumption – consumption by desirable consumers. That's the area where most brand marketers are not just deficient, it's the great black void of knowledge they currently face.

Recognizing the change in brand marketing and communication value from what is sent out to what is consumed, Schultz and Pilotta (2004) and Schultz, Pilotta and Block (2005, 2006) began to develop

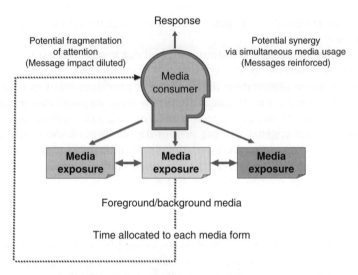

Figure 3.4   Media consumption model
Source: Schultz and Pilotta, ESOMAR 2004.

a methodology by which consumer media usage and media consumption patterns could be identified, measured and evaluated. The general model they developed is illustrated in Figure 3.4.

Rather than starting with what the marketer sends out through various 'push media' forms, the consumption model starts with what marketing and communication activities and elements consumers either access or to which they expose themselves. (Exposure simply means the consumer spends time with the media form and, assuming the marketer employs that media form, the consumer at least has an opportunity-to-see-or-hear the marketers brand messages or receive their incentives). When starting with media consumption, brand marketers must first determine what media form or forms the consumer accesses. Then, the challenge is to identify how much time consumers are allocating to each media form and, finally, whether the media form is primary, that is, currently being processed or in the background, that is, simply being monitored.

The key element in this consumption measurement process is time, that is, how much time is spent with each media form. The premise is that the consumer, with limited available time, uses the media form or forms which they believe to be the most important to them, whether that is to gather marketplace information or simply for entertainment. In either case, if they personally access the media form, the likelihood of media involvement is substantially enhanced.

The primary advantage of this consumption model is that almost all traditional media measures involve the amount or number of messages or incentives distributed through that media form, that is, number of commercials broadcast, newspapers or magazines printed, autos passing an outdoor sign and so on. The same is being done with many of the new interactive media. Web owners and other service providers identify the websites accessed, on which ones the consumer clicked or to what other websites they transitioned, what search engine was employed and so on. So, even though the new interactive and online media forms have consumer interactions, they still generally lack a feedback loop which would enable the marketer to trace online exposures to more relevant consumer activities such as follow-on sales. So, in spite of the interactive nature of the new online media, it's still difficult to measure marketing and communication results, particularly brands and branding at much more relevant levels beyond simple message exposure.

The bigger brand marketing and communication measurement question today, however, is not just which or what media form the consumer accessed or used, but to what combination of media they exposed themselves to or which ones they accessed. Simultaneous media usage (SIMM) is rampant today around the world. Consumers are often online, watching television, flipping through a magazine and talking on a cell phone, all at the same time. When one considers that brand marketers practically never go to market with just one promotional tool, that is advertising alone or Web search alone or mobile alone, the question then becomes: What media forms consumers are using together and in what combinations? Knowing those combinations is the key element in brand marketing and communication today. Those combinations provide major brand marketing and communication insights for future planning.

These two factors, (a) the need for media consumption data and (b) media combination measures, led to the development of the BIGresearch SIMM studies. These new media planning resources and the capabilities they produce are in the next section.

3   The Simultaneous Media Usage studies

Recognizing the changing media marketplace brought on by simultaneous media usage, in 2002, BIGresearch, Columbus, OH (www.bigresearch.com), began a series of twice-yearly online studies on consumer reported media usage and other data in the United States. Similar media consumption studies have been conducted in China on a quarterly basis since 2006. (All data in this chapter is based on the US studies unless expressly stated otherwise.)

Called the SIMM studies, there are now 15 nationally projectable samples with approximately 17,000–20,000 responses in each wave, that is, now over 200,000 individual responses in the database. In each SIMM study, which is based on accepted online data gathering techniques, respondents are asked to provide information on their media usage on an average day in both minutes used and form of media accessed. Thirty-one media forms are tracked ranging from television (both over the air and cable) to newspapers to email to in-store promotions. The depth and breadth of the SIMM data thus enables a full view of consumer media usage, both online and offline, as respondents provide details on media forms used and the amount of time for each of them. In addition, respondents report what media forms are used in what combinations, that is, when a person is online, are they also attending to television or flipping through a magazine or talking on a cell phone.

A key question in the ongoing studies is: What is the influence of the media form on your purchase behaviors in each of the nine product categories tracked, that is, apparel/clothing, automobiles/trucks, eating out, electronics, financial services, grocery, home improvement, medicines and telecommunications/wireless. With this set of data, it is possible to identify which media forms are most widely used and which are most influential by product category. In addition, since consumers also report their favorite retailer for each of the product categories, researchers are also able to identify the media usage by favored retailer. Thus, it is possible to build models based on the connections between the product category and the store customers and how they compare and contrast. In summary, the SIMM studies are likely one of the most comprehensive views of media consumption in the United States today.

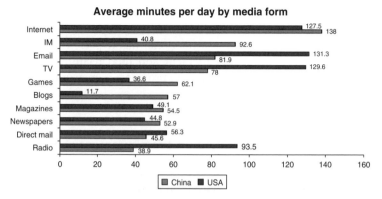

Figure 3.5   Comparison of Chinese and US media usage

Source: China: 1st Quarter, 2008 – BIGresearch, Inc.

US: 1st Half 2008 – BIGresearch, Inc.

The ongoing gathering of media consumption data in the United States and China also enables a comparison to be made between how US consumers use the various media forms and how those same media forms are used by Chinese consumers. An example of that type of comparison is shown as Figure 3.5.

Clearly, media consumption varies considerably between the United States and China with US consumers much more focused on traditional media while the Chinese opt for the new digital forms such as instant messaging, blogs, online games and the like. This new type of media consumption is changing how marketers must consider their global brand marketing and communication planning and measurement in this transformational period of marketing. What works in one country may not work in another, thus, the opportunity for global brand marketing and communication programs may only be an empty dream and not really possible in practice.

The SIMM studies are being shared with approximately ten US universities and several schools overseas for research purposes. The analyses contained in this chapter are the result of the media consumption studies conducted by the faculty in the Integrated Marketing Communications Department at Northwestern University, Evanston, IL, USA.

The SIMM data forms the base for the new brand media allocation and measurement models which follow. First, however, it is important to connect the new transformational marketplace to the need for media consumption measurement and then relate that to the promotion of brands and branding to provide a framework for what follows.

4   How brand management and measurement change in the transformational marketplace

While brands and branding have been used for millennia, the study of brands as a marketing phenomenon is fairly recent. The first major text to cover the subject of brands and branding in the modern marketplace was published by Aaker in 1991. So, while there is a long history of brands and branding, our formalized knowledge is limited. Yet, brands and branding will likely be one of the key elements in the evolving transformational marketplace. Many argue that the brand will be the primary differentiating factor. The reason? Almost all products and services and even organizations are increasingly becoming commoditized. Thus, connecting brand basics to the requirements of the radically different marketplace becomes critical. A brief review of brands and branding, and how those relate to the new marketplace, follows.

The first issue in any brand discussion is simply: What is a brand? There are many definitions. We put the question into perspective through the schematic in Figure 3.6.

Clearly, the brand is not one single element, but a combination of the specific trademarks, bundles of intellectual property owned by the organization and, finally, the branded business itself, which is what most marketers mean when they say 'the brand'. The key issue is that, internally, the organization must be clear about what they mean by the term 'brand'. That's the first step when developing any type of brand communication measurement program. For discussion purposes, the highest level brand definition, that is, the branded business is used in this discussion.

Using this brand definition, the question of how brand marketing and communication can or will be used to establish, enhance or maintain the brand asset in the marketplace becomes much easier.

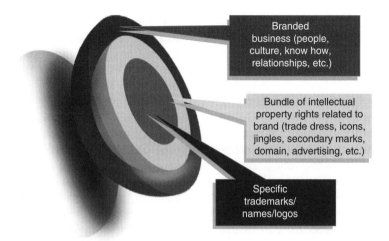

Figure 3.6 What is a brand?
Source: Brand Finance, LLC.

Historically, broad-scale marketing and communication using mass media have been the primary tools used to build brand awareness and interest among consumers. So, when 'brand building communication' is mentioned, it generally refers to traditional outbound brand communication programs initiated by the marketing organization. Those are the activities the brand owners have used to attempt to embed brand concepts in the minds of the consumer.

Brand communication, therefore, was traditionally developed and delivered by the brand owner through various forms of outbound, generally media-delivered communication systems. Therefore, most of our brand building knowledge and experience is based on the advertising, promotion, events or other activities the brand-owning organization developed and distributed in the marketplace. Since the brand owner and manager had specific concepts or ideas, which they believed properly proscribed the brand concepts and messages they owned, brand communication programs were carefully developed, sharply honed and then sent out to customers and prospects. Because brand consumers had limited access to alternative views, and limited communication systems with other consumers, the marketer was generally able to control the broad-scale images of the brand. In other words, the outbound communication from the brand owner was generally the only image the consumer had of the brand outside of their own experience. Indeed, the typical brand communication system of the past half-century very closely resembled the outbound 'push communication' system illustrated earlier in Figure 3.2.

The development of interactive media forms, however, has resulted in an explosion of media venues through which brand communication can occur. That includes both outbound and inbound, push and pull and by both the marketer and the consumer. The big change in brand marketing and brand communication, however, has been the consumer's newly found capability to 'talk back' or to comment on the marketing activities of the marketer, particularly the brand messaging the marketing organization is trying to deliver. These online systems, particularly the social networks, make the brand much more transparent and less protected and, therefore, more vulnerable to consumer comments and reactions, which can be either laudatory or damning. It's this newly developed marketplace brand image vulnerability that really signals the change in how the brand must be managed in the transformational marketplace.

The most challenging situation faced by brand owners and managers are the increasingly large numbers of people who can impact the brand and its marketplace value simply by commenting on the brand through the various interactive marketing and communication channels. Where once the marketer could clearly identify the target markets and limit the brand communication programs to specific groups of people and geographies, today, the depth and range of the brand's communication activities and audiences is a major challenge. Figure 3.7 illustrates the changes in brand communication the manager faces today in most brand marketing organizations.

Two extremely important factors now impact the brand in the transformational marketplace. The first is that brand communication, that is communication the marketing organization traditionally sent out to audiences through various communication systems, has given way to the much broader concept of brand experiences. Brands no longer are built or maintained simply through brand communication. Instead, brands live or die based on the experiences consumers or brand users have with them. And, those come from a broad variety of sources. Only a few are shown in the Figure but they are representative of the type of experiences consumers and other brand audiences

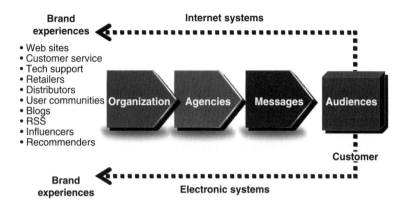

Figure 3.7 Online brand experiences occur

have with everything from customer service to websites to external blogs. All add to or detract from the brand image the marketer is trying to build for his or her brand.

The major challenge, of course, is that in too many cases, the people or groups delivering the brand messages and incentives today have simply not been trained to do so. They have no background, knowledge or experience as brand ambassadors, yet that is essentially what they are, that is, on-the-spot, surrogate brand managers or brand advocates, who are more closely associated with brand success than the formal brand managers inside the corporate organization. It is this diffusion of capabilities and responsibilities that really defines the new transitional system for brands and brand communication.

The second point in Figure 3.7 is that the brand experiences customers or brand users receive generally occur behind or outside the brand marketing organization itself. Too often today, brand managers don't really know the type of experiences customers and consumers are having with their brand or brands and they have few ways to learn about them. Thus, one of the key elements in managing or building brands in the transformational marketplace is simply that brand experience and brand communication consumption will become even more critical to long-term brand success. That means, new methods and approaches to brand communication development and new measures of brand communication success will be needed. Those are the challenges for brand marketing and communication, much more than simply enhancing or improving the processes presently in place.

As a result of these changes in consumer power over the brand, it becomes increasingly important to understand brand communication consumption models, not just brand distribution models. In the SIMM data, the broad range of media forms, their consumption and usage by respondents and the influence they have on brand purchase behaviors does much to help us truly understand what is important in brand marketing and communication.

A key point in this 'push and pull communication system' is how the brand must be managed. Recently, both Procter & Gamble (2009) and Unilever (2009) have announced new brand management systems. Both these branding giants have moved away from organizational models based on internal brand structures to ones that focus on communicating with specific, identifiable brand audiences quickly and continuously. Clearly, this change will require a focus on brand message consumption by those audiences, rather than the broader-based brand communication methodologies of the past.

Similarly, Forrester Research in a recent study argued (2009) that 'brand managers' are no longer relevant since they imply the ability of the brand owner to control brand messages and brand images. Instead, the research organization suggests a transformation of brand managers into 'brand advocates' who, Forrester says, will be in charge of the 'heart and soul of what the brand stands for'. In the new, transformed brand communication scenario of today and tomorrow, Forrester suggests that the role of those 'brand advocates' will be to respond as quickly as possible to changing consumer trends based on customer insights and market research using 'predictive modeling' rather than the historical data which has traditionally been used in brand management. The use of SIMM data to develop predictive models is discussed in Sections 6–8.

Further, Forrester suggests that smaller, more frequent forms of brand communication, over a wider number of platforms, will be preferable to the traditional major 'bursts' of activity in the mass media once or twice a year. That follows well with the quickly fragmenting media marketplace which is all around us. All these changes further verify the argument being made in this chapter that brand marketing and communication are changing and must change to be relevant in the transformational marketplace.

With this view of brands and branding, we can now move to a more detailed discussion of media consumption and with that, examples and explanations of how media consumption approaches, using the SIMM data, can radically change, how marketing and communication must be conducted and measured in the transformational marketplace.

5 The three key elements in media consumption

Drawing on SIMM study data, four key elements have been identified which help explain the new measurement systems for brand marketing and communication in the transformational marketplace. Those are (a) the media form(s) consumers choose to access and use; (b) the amount of time they spend with each of those media forms in minutes per day; (c) the media forms used in combination, that is, which ones are used together, that is, simultaneously and (d) which media forms consumers report as having the most influence on their future purchasing decisions. Thus, one of the primary differences in the media consumption approach to marketing and communication measurement is that SIMM data enables the marketer to develop a set of predictive models of future consumer behavior based on their media consumption. Longitudinal studies show what consumers have done in the past and the probability is the same will occur in the future. The law of large numbers, that is, the 200,000+ responses to the SIMM questionnaires, further validates the general trends and smoothes out outlier responses by respondents which creates very accurate predictions.

The four measures listed above are discussed below.

1. Media Form Selected or Accessed

   The basic premise of any media consumption measure is that consumers allocate their most precious asset, time, to the media forms they believe have the most relevance and value to them. Given the wide array of alternatives, there is no reason for a consumer to waste his or her time with a media form that does not provide some value, however, fleeting. Thus, the first measure in the media consumption studies is for consumers to identify which media forms they use from the list of 31 alternatives measured in the SIMM studies (see Appendix A for a list of the media forms measured).

2. Amount of Time Spent With Each Media Form

The second key element is the amount of time spent with each media form in an average day. Given there are 1440 minutes in a 24-hour day, this time allocation is a further indication of which media form or forms the consumer considers important. The actual question in the survey asks respondents to provide the amount of time in minutes spent with each medium during an average day. Further, those time allocations are made on the basis of broadcast time segments, that is, prime time, early evening, morning drive and so on. That enables a comparison with traditional media time measures if needed.

Figure 3.8 combines the media form(s) used and the amount of time spent with each form each day to illustrate the approach.

In this example, the average minutes per day by medium data has been aggregated for all product categories found in the First Quarter, 2008 SIMM study. This chart combines all nine product categories and provides an overview of the total reported data. In the example, Email leads in the amount of time spent, followed by Television and then the Internet. Thus, the electronic media account for a preponderance of all media usage during this SIMM study period.

	Avg Minutes per Day
Email	131.3
TV	129.6
Internet	127.5
Radio	93.5
Direct	56.3
Magazines	49.1
Newspaper	44.8
IM	40.8
Games	36.6
Satellite	22.0
Web Radio	14.4
Blog	11.7

Figure 3.8   Measures #1 and #2 – How much time consumers spend with each media form

Source: First Quarter, 2008, BIGresearch.

3. Combinations of Media Forms Used Simultaneously
   A critical measure in media consumption is what media forms
   are consumed together, that is, simultaneously. Clearly, consumers multitask with media today. Therefore, the key question
   is what media forms they use together. That becomes a primary
   element for brand marketer when trying to make measurable
   brand media investment decisions. Figure 3.9 illustrates how
   these media combinations can be viewed together in a matrix
   format.
   The most common media usage is a combination of television and online. In this example, 37.5 percent of the respondents
   who reported they were online also said they were watching or
   involved with television, simultaneously. Reading down, online is
   the primary medium, with television being the secondary or sup-
   plementary media form. When the question is reversed, that is,
   'when you're watching television what other media form are you
   also using?', the figure across is 26 percent, that is, number in one
   sample who said they were also online. This shift between the primary and secondary media forms further illustrates the concept of
   'foreground' and 'background' media, discussed earlier. People are
   actually creating their own media agendas today and that likely
   will only increase in the future.

Primary medium (when ..., do you simultaneously ....)
(regularly only)

	Online	TV	Maga-zines	News-papers	Direct mail	Cell phone	Radio
Online		26.2	6.1	8.1	9.9	13.9	17.1
TV	37.5		20.2	24.1	21.4	14.9	8.0
Magazines	7.0	10.3				5.0	8.3
Newspaper	10.3	11.6				4.7	11.3
Direct mail	21.0	14.2				6.7	10.7
Radio	21.7	3.8	11.8	12.6	12.2	11.7	

Figure 3.9 Measure #3 – Media combinations
Source: 1st Quarter, 2008 – BIGresearch, Inc.

4. Influence of Media Form on Purchase Decisions

Perhaps the most critical element in understanding brand media consumption is the consumer's reporting of what media form has or had the most influence in their purchasing decisions. That information is shown in Figure 3.10.

In the figure, eight of the nine product categories reported in the SIMM data are aggregated to provide an overview of the concept of purchase influence. The percentages shown are the percentage of the SIMM study respondents for the first half of 2008 study. In this example, Word-of-Mouth is the most influential media form, followed by Coupons, Inserts and then Television. What is most interesting is the highly promotional nature of the US marketplace since Coupons and Inserts (Sunday free-standing and other inserts in the daily newspaper) are commonly filled with money-saving or reduced price offers. We do not find this same interest in Coupons and Inserts in the Chinese studies.

The importance of this media consumption approach becomes apparent when the data is used either as a media planning tool or as a method of evaluating and measuring the impact of the organization's marketing and communication expenditures. Historically, since most media measurement has been based on (a) individual media forms, that is, television is measured separately

	% Influence		% Influence
Word-of-Mouth	36.2	Radio	13.1
Coupons	28.4	Internet	12.3
Inserts	21.5	Email	11.7
TV	20.8	Outdoor	7.2
Newspapers	20.0	Yellow Pages	7.0
Read Article	19.8	Blog	3.1
In-Store	19.6	Satellite	3.1
Direct	19.1	IM	2.9
Magazines	17.0	Web Radio	2.7
Cable	13.6	Picture Phone	2.2

*Across 8 product categories, Apparel/Clothing, Automobile, Eating Out, Electronics, Grocery, Home Improvement, Medicines, and Telecom/Wireless

Figure 3.10   Measure #4 – Influence media form has on consumer purchase decisions

Source: 1st Half, 2008 – BIGresearch, Inc.

from radio which is counted separately from outdoor and so on, which is then factored against (b) the distribution of messages and incentives only, with no assurance that they were consumed at all, and, (c) the lack of information on which media form has the most, if any influence, on past or future purchasing decisions, the value of media consumption becomes very clear.

From this media consumption data, three new brand measurement and evaluation approaches have emerged. Those are discussed in the next three sections.

6   Media consumption data Use #1 – Validating media planning decisions

Historically, the measurement of brand marketing activities, particularly the media portion of those measures, has been on confirming whether or not the messages and incentives the marketer purchased were actually distributed. Thus, one of the current key measures in marketing and communication today is simply media distribution confirmation. This becomes as much a check on distribution as a value measure, but it is still one of the more critical media measures relied on by both agencies and marketers.

A much more important measure in the transformational marketplace is whether or not the right audience was selected initially and whether or not the messages and incentives were placed in the media forms the target audience actually use. This is where media consumption makes a big difference. The following example illustrates the concept.

Assume a marketer wants to reach the Hispanic market in the United States. A wide variety of media forms are available, some in English and some in Spanish. Presently, from a message brand communication distribution view, the only alternatives are based on the estimated audiences for the various media alternatives, yet often little is known as to whether the consumer would prefer English or Spanish language. That's where media consumption becomes an important factor.

In the June, 2008 SIMM study, a total of 16,187 consumer responses were generated. Of those responders, 13.8 percent were from people who said they were Hispanic. That's approximately the same percentage as the US Census estimates. More important, however, is the question of whether these respondents prefer their media in Spanish or English. Again, drawing on SIMM media consumption data, in the Hispanic group, the five most important Spanish-language media forms are:

Internet	10.8%
Newspapers	15.7%
Radio	17.3%
Magazines	18.5%
Television	23.8%

Interestingly, in every major media, less than 25 percent of the SIMM Hispanic sample prefer the use of Spanish-language media. Thus, in many instances, reaching the Hispanic market can be accomplished with the proper selection of English-language media. Yet, the group preferring Spanish-language may be very important to the marketer.

To determine the importance of Spanish-language media, media consumption is a primary brand planning tool. The amount of time the Hispanic consumers said they spent with Spanish-language media is shown in Figure 3.11.

The number of minutes of Hispanic respondents who prefer Spanish-language media is compared to those of other Hispanics who prefer English-language media. Therefore, responses by media

	Hispanic	Other	Total	Hispanic Index
Internet	128.25	128.20	126.47	101.4
TV	126.78	133.23	130.78	96.9
Email	120.67	134.57	131.14	92.0
Radio	90.14	92.86	92.17	97.8
Direct Mail	57.34	56.58	56.38	101.7
IM	54.61	37.71	39.75	137.4
Magazines	49.67	49.30	49.02	101.3
Games	44.95	36.57	37.02	121.4
Newspaper	44.39	46.19	45.76	97.0
Web Radio	22.06	12.85	14.16	155.8
Satellite	21.88	23.17	22.83	95.8
Blogs	18.20	10.35	11.25	161.8

Figure 3.11   Spanish vs English media usage

form have been indexed. From this, a totally different picture of the Hispanic market emerges.

While the amount of time spent by Spanish-language preferring Hispanic respondents still strongly favor the Internet, TV and Email, the less visible media of Instant Messaging, Games, Web Radio and Blogs index much higher in terms of the amount of time Spanish-language consumers' use with them. That is further shown in Figure 3.12 which combines Amount of Time Spent and Media Influence.

In this chart, Spanish-language preference, Time Spent with the Media Form and Influence of the Media Form in Purchasing Decisions have all been combined. What is clearly evident is the heavy involvement of Spanish-language preferring consumers with all forms of new, online media. Using only the index figures, the top-rated media in terms of influence are: Instant Messaging, Video on Cell Phones, Web Radio, Text Messaging, Games and Blogs. Clearly, the Spanish-speaking Hispanic community is greatly interested in many of the

	Hispanic	Other	Total	Hispanic Index
Word of Mouth	33.39	35.92	35.39	94.3
Coupons	25.63	27.76	27.43	93.4
TV	24.55	19.74	20.32	120.9
In-store	21.61	18.81	19.09	113.2
Magazines	21.07	16.03	16.71	126.1
Newspapers	20.31	20.62	20.54	98.9
Direct Mail	20.06	18.87	18.90	106.1
Inserts	19.81	21.68	21.30	93.0
Cable	18.06	12.71	13.34	135.4
Read an Article	18.00	20.14	19.65	91.6
Internet	16.63	11.30	11.94	139.2
Radio	15.20	12.35	12.72	119.5
Email	14.21	10.98	11.36	125.1
Product Placement	11.97	8.42	8.80	136.0
Outdoor	10.93	6.43	6.99	156.2
Yellow Pages	8.45	6.92	7.09	119.3
IM	5.86	2.34	2.82	207.4
Blog	5.34	2.74	3.06	174.6
Web Radio	4.98	2.23	2.63	189.7
Text	4.69	2.07	2.42	194.2
Satellite	4.52	2.92	3.16	143.2
Games	4.37	2.07	2.36	184.7
Video on Cell	4.32	1.80	2.15	201.2

Figure 3.12 Time and average media influence

forms of new media, particularly those which are available in the Spanish language. So, while traditional media still dominate usage time, and, in some cases, even the influence measures, reaching the Spanish-speaking Hispanic community in the United States may well be enhanced through non-traditional media forms such as the new electronic media.

Without media consumption data, it is unlikely a marketer would have been able to determine these types of media influence on their target market in a transformational marketplace.

The added value of this type of media consumption data is that it provides a way for organizations to focus their communication efforts against relatively small, but often very important, consumer audiences that would normally have simply slipped under their radar. As marketing and communication increasingly becomes more and more 'audience specific and relevant', media consumption data becomes increasingly important to brand marketers.

While this type of customer information is very useful, it is still calculated 'after-the-fact', that is, a comparison is made of what was done with what could have been done. The decision has been made and the money is gone. Much more important going forward will be the development of a predictive brand media allocation approach to help marketers identify what media forms they should use going forward. That's next.

7   Media consumption data Use #2 – Fine tuning message and incentive allocation with predictive models

One of the key elements in the transformational brand marketing and communication marketplace will be the demand for predictive models of the optimal brand marketing and communication investment. The historical approach of sending out brand messages and incentives, and then, measuring the returns after-the-fact is simply not practical in the fragmented, rapidly changing transformational marketplace. The marketplace is simply too fluid to wait for marketplace results. Further, given the wide array of marketing and communication alternatives, optimization models likely lose their relevance as well. The media permutations are simply too great to adequately determine optimal message distribution. That means, the marketer must be more attuned than ever to what likely response will be generated as a result of a brand marketing or communication investments. And the solution is predictive modeling.

Predictive modeling is simply a method of identifying or estimating in advance what media forms could or should be used to create the most impact through future brand investments. Media consumption data can substantially improve this type of allocation. And, as the number of brand marketing and communication alternatives literally explode, the value of identifying forecasted results grows exponentially.

One of the values of knowing potential consumer media consumption is that it allows the marketer to constrain the number of alternative promotional choices to be considered. If the number of alternative choices can be winnowed down, the probability of making the right one improves substantially. That's the second change in developing an alternative approach to allocating and measuring brand marketing and communication in the transformational marketplace.

One of the key elements in the SIMM data is the question to consumers about 'What major purchases are you considering making in the next six months'. Note, these are considered purchases, not those bought regularly as replenishments of consumable products. These are things the consumer has in mind and is planning toward such as an automobile, a television set, real estate or the category used in the following example, a personal computer.

In the June, 2008 SIMM study, 15.19 percent of the sample respondents said they were planning on purchasing a personal computer in the next 6 months. That provided the framework of 'intended purchasers'. Using the SIMM data, this purchase intent was then combined with the media forms those same consumers said has the greatest influence on them in the Electronics product category. The results of that analysis is shown in Figure 3.13.

Note first, those respondents saying they planned on buying a computer in the next 6 months have higher overall media usage than those not planning to buy. That has been found in a number of SIMM studies. If people are in the market for major products, they often spend more time with the media, apparently monitoring for product information and offerings.

The second thing is the high incidence of 'promotional media forms', that is, Coupons, Inserts, Newspapers and so on being used.

Do you plan to make a computer purchase within the next 6 months by Media Influence?

	No	Yes	Total
Coupons	26.8	31.0	27.4
Inserts	20.6	25.0	21.3
Newspapers	19.8	24.7	20.5
TV	19.2	26.8	20.3
In-Store	18.3	23.3	19.1
Direct	18.2	23.1	18.9
Magazines	15.6	22.7	16.7
Cable	12.3	19.3	13.3
Radio	11.7	18.5	12.7
Internet	10.6	19.3	11.9
Email	10.4	16.8	11.4
Yellow Pages	6.5	10.5	7.1
Outdoor	6.3	11.0	7.0

Figure 3.13   Purchase intent and media influence

Source: SIMM, June 2008.

All are commonly sources of promotional programs for personal computers. In other words, people who are planning to buy are looking for the best value and one of the resources they use is the media.

In Figure 3.13, 13 of the 31 media forms are shown. While the figure is interesting and helpful in knowing consumer media usage, sorting through 13 alternatives is still a difficult task. To help reduce the manager's investment choices, a CHAID (Chi Square Automatic Interaction Detection) tree analysis was conducted. CHAID is a statistical analytic tool commonly used in direct marketing applications. The computer program first identifies the one factor which contributes the most to explaining the alternatives shown in Figure 3.13. It then proceeds to identify the explanatory variables on the basis of which one has the greatest value, then the next, and so on down the list of variables. A 'tree' with 'branches' is thus created. This shows the relationship among and between all the variables being considered. The output of the CHAID analysis is commonly a fairly large matrix. The CHAID tree above has been 'pruned' to show the most important factors as in Figure 3.14.

In the SIMM sample, from which this chart was constructed, 15.19 percent of the respondents said they planned on buying a computer in the next 6 months. The media form which explained the greatest media influence was Internet usage. Internet usage was then split into High, Low and No Internet Usage. For those with High Internet

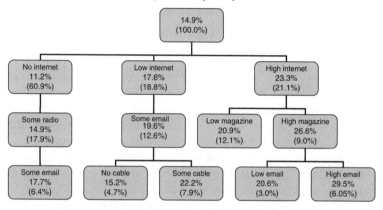

Plan to buy a computer by categories of media influence
Total plan to buy computer

Figure 3.14 Pruned CHAID tree
Source: SIMM, June 2008.

Usage, the next most important media variable was Magazines. This was split into High and Low Usage. For those who were not using the Internet, the next highest predicting variable was Some Radio. The same 'treeing' was done for the other predictor variables as shown.

By using this one chart, the brand marketer now knows, in advance of committing any money, the media forms which have the highest probability of reaching prospective computer purchasers. For High Internet Users, that would be the addition of Magazines and Email. For those with No Internet, the best alternatives would be Radio and Email. Thus, the computer brand marketer now has a 'predictive media contact' methodology to assist in identifying the media form or forms which consumers intending to buy a computer would likely use. Therefore, the brand's media plan could be developed in advance of the media buy, something which becomes very critical in the transformational marketplace of almost unlimited brand communication channels and rapidly changing consumer markets.

While this type of predictive modeling will undoubtedly improve the allocation of brand resources, it is just as important to determine what has occurred in the past so that predictive brand communication programs to be used in the future can be enhanced and improved. That follows in the next section.

8   Media consumption data Use #3 – Replacing current ROI models with allocation and planning algorithms

Currently, the focus of most brand marketing and communication measurement is on ROI (Return-on-Investment). This is an accounting term which has been shifted to marketing and brand measurement. It simply means: what did we get back for what we spent. The problem, of course, is that directly connecting investments in brand marketing and communication activities to sales results is extremely difficult to do. The reason: brand marketing and communication generally don't generate immediate returns, that is, those occurring in the present fiscal period. Thus, while a number of alternative ROI and other measurement systems have been developed, ranging from Attitudinal Shifts to Marketing Mix Modeling (econometric analysis to try to control for all the sales and return variables), the success of these approaches has become quite tenuous. The primary challenge, of course, is that most of the evaluation models rely on historical data, something that is proving to be less and less relevant in the turbulent markets of the past few years. Clearly a better approach is needed.

If the marketer knows the media consumption of those planning to purchase in a particular product category in the next few months, as in the computer illustration above, then better models of brand communication allocation can be developed. Thus, an argument is made that in the transformational marketplace, the proper allocation of brand communication resources is a much more critical decision than attempting to measure the results after the resources have already been spent. While this seems like a truism, in most investigations of budgeting and allocation, few if any relevant models can be found. Thus, the opportunity to improve allocation with media consumption becomes very relevant.

In the example below, data from the 2007–2008 SIMM studies have been combined to illustrate the principles involved. We draw our example from the always interesting automobile category.

First, the brand communication investments by the top seven automobile manufacturers (Note: these are automobile manufacturers,

2007 Auto advertisers (top seven) among top 100 media spending – advertising age – TNS

	Millions of dollars	Percent
Magazines	1,507	18.4
Newspapers	538	6.6
Outdoor	119	1.5
TV	5,206	63.6
Radio	252	3.1
Internet	558	6.8
Measured media	8,180	100.0

Figure 3.15 Spending by the top seven automobile brands
Source: Top 100 National Advertisers, Advertising Age, 2008.

not specific name plates. Name plates were aggregated up to the corporate entity) were determined. These came from TNS figures, published in *Advertising Age* (2008).

The top seven brand promotional forms are shown in Figure 3.15 for 2007 in terms of the spending by the total automobile category. As can be seen, television received the preponderance of all promotional investments, followed by magazines and so on. This is how the automobile companies actually spent their money. The question is: Was there a better way to invest those brand resources?

Again, using the TNS data, the Share-Of-Voice of each of the auto manufacturers as a percentage of all auto manufacturer's spending was calculated. That was done simply by taking the spending by each auto marketer and dividing it by the total spend in the category. That is shown in Figure 3.16 as 'SOV%'. General Motors had the highest Share-of-Voice or spending share in the category with 24.2 percent. Other auto companies were calculated and the SOV are shown.

That SOV calculation was then combined with data from the June, 2008 SIMM study. There, we took the number of survey respondents who selected each of the auto manufacturers as providing their first choice among all automobiles. That is shown as '1st Choice %'. General Motors led in first choice with 26.2 percent preference.

From that, a simple ratio of SOV vs 1st Choice was determined. All that is shown in Figure 3.16.

2007 Auto share of voice* and reported first choice in next 6 months**

	SOV %	1st Choice %	Ratio
General motors corp.	24.2	26.2	1.08
Ford motor co.	20.3	17.9	.88
Toyota motor corp.	14.1	18.0	1.27
Chrysler	14.0	13.3	0.95
Nissan motor co.	11.4	7.0	0.62
Honda motor co.	10.7	14.9	1.40
Hyundai motor co.	5.2	2.6	0.49

*2007 TNS based on the seven manufacturers
**Includes all brands for each manufacturer and excludes other manufacturers
    brands, SIMM June '08

Figure 3.16   Share-Of-Voice by SIMM 1st choice reports

From Figure 3.16, it can be seen that Honda and Toyota were get-ting the most 'bang for their bucks' in terms of their promotional spending. That is, their consumer preference or Choice exceeded their Share-Of-Voice spending. Hyundai promotion delivered the weakest impact on purchase preference.

Next, using the industry standard estimates of Cost-Per-Thousand (CPM) delivered messages, which are shown in Figure 3.17, we devel-oped another analysis. These range from $7.35 for Outdoor to $9.00 for Blogs and Satellite Radio and up to $33.18 for Newspapers. From this, an Influence Points per Thousand ratio was determined. This was simply a calculation using the industry-determined CPM costs and comparing those to the Media Influence percentage by promo-tional form from the SIMM data. Thus, the Influence Points per $1000 of Spending was determined.

The Influence Points/$1000 ranged from a low of 1.30 for Prod-uct Placement to a high of 13.45 for Magazines. This, we believe, is a much more valuable calculation than the Share-Of-Voice shown earlier which has often been used in brand marketing and communi-cation reviews.

All the preceding calculations and estimates have been based on the total SIMM respondent base. Unfortunately, that is what is com-monly done in brand marketing and communication planning today

	CPM ($)	Influence	Influence Points/$1000
Magazines	12.68	17.05	13.45
Inserts	16.00	21.49	13.43
Outdoor	7.35	7.28	9.88
Radio	14.43	13.08	9.06
Internet	15.33	12.33	8.04
TV	26.84	20.89	7.78
Newspapers	33.18	19.98	6.02
E-Mail	20.00	11.73	5.87
Blogs	9.00	3.17	3.52
Satellite	9.00	3.13	3.48
Product placement	70.00	9.10	1.30

Figure 3.17   Cost weighted by influence
Source: SIMM, June 2008.

as well. That is, a non-prospective buyer is given the same weight as one who has already signified his or her intent to buy in the category in upcoming months. Using the June, 2008 SIMM study, it was next determined that approximately 11.4 percent of the sample signified they planned on purchasing a car or truck in the next 6 months. Thus, a far more relevant number for any automobile brand Marketing planning or investments would be based on that group.

In Figure 3.18, all the SIMM data is combined. That is the Media Influence for all respondents in the SIMM study (All Auto Influence) is compared to those respondents saying they planned to buy in the next 6 months (Planner Influence). Media Usage, that is the amount of time spent with each of the media/promotional forms, that is, TV = 139.0 minutes per day, Newspaper = 54.1 minutes per day and so on, is also shown. The fourth column is the Cost-per-Thousand (CPM) from Figure 3.17.

The figures in Figure 3.18, provide the data for the two final analyses of the Auto Promotional Allocation approach which can be created from the SIMM media consumption studies.

	All auto influence	Planner influence	Usage	CPM
TV	21.4	31.0	139.0	26.84
Newspapers	19.6	29.2	54.1	33.18
Magazines	16.1	25.8	58.4	12.68
Radio	14.2	22.9	102.0	14.43
Internet	10.7	18.5	147.3	15.33
Outdoor	10.3	17.2	14.4	7.35

Figure 3.18 Media form influence on planned buyers
Source: Media Generations.

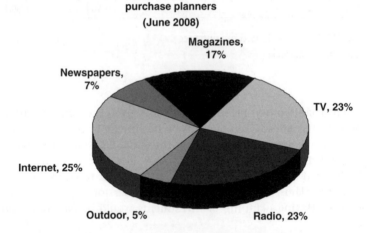

Optimal dollar allocation for car and truck purchase planners (June 2008)

Magazines, 17%

Newspapers, 7%

TV, 23%

Internet, 25%

Outdoor, 5%

Radio, 23%

Figure 3.19 Optimal media allocation for planned purchasers
Source: SIMM, June 2008.

Figure 3.19 is a calculation of the Optimal Media Allocation of Brand Promotional Resources for Planned Automobile Purchasers. Combining the Planner Influence, the Media Usage and the CPM figures from Figure 3.18, the optimal percentage allocation of resources for all manufacturer brands in the automobile category has been determined. As shown, if the focus is on the media form most preferred by and used by respondents to make an automobile

Comparison of car and truck manufacturer advertising*
and the optimal allocation 2007 $**

	2007 $**	%	Optimal $	%	Change $
Internet	558	6.8	2,079	25.4	1,521
Radio	252	3.1	1.891	23.1	1,639
TV	5,206	63.6	1,874	22.9	−3,332
Magazines	1,507	18.4	1,386	16.9	−121
Newspapers	538	6.6	556	6.8	18
Outdoor	119	1.5	393	4.8	274

*Top 7 auto advertisers from top 100 list
**Millions

Figure 3.20 Comparison of past car advertising allocation to optimal investment

purchase decision, the optimal amount for Television would have been 23 percent of the available dollars, 17 percent would have gone to Magazines, 23 percent to Radio and so on.

The optimal allocation takes into account the impact and influence of the various media forms, the amount of time spent with each of them by the prospective purchasers and the cost of the media form (CPM). Thus, by re-constructing the media allocation model which actually occurred in 2007, where overspending and where under-spending occurred can be determined. That is shown in Figure 3.20.

In Figure 3.20, the actual 2007 spending by the automobile manufacturers is compared to the optimal amount as determined by three of the four factors previously discussed, that is, (a) the media forms selected by the consumers, (b) the amount of time spent with each media form and (c) the influence of the media form on the upcoming purchase decision. The promotional costs by alternative have been added to this to generate the 'over-and-under-spend' chart shown above.

Perhaps the most important figure in the calculation above is the estimate of the actual dollar mis-allocation. For example, using the SIMM data and brand media consumption estimates, the auto makers overspent by $3.3 billion in television and under-spent by $1.639

billion in Radio and $1.521 billion in Internet. Clearly, if automobile manufacturers focused on their prospective customers, rather than the calculus presently being used, radically different media allocation results would occur. The question, of course, is: Would the reallocation of these brand resources to this optimal model have made a difference in the returns the automobile marketers received on their investments? At this point, no one can say. But, what one can say is that with media consumption approaches such as those found in the SIMM data, the automobile manufacturers could certainly have aligned their investments much better with prospect preferences than they did in 2007.

The importance of these examples and illustrations shows that media consumption is a critical variable going forward. As brand marketers move forward in the transformational marketplace, the approaches demonstrated must play a much more important role in brand marketing and communication. There is increasingly solid evidence that better allocation will likely result in better returns or ROI.

Budgeting and allocation for brand marketing is likely one of the most critical issues faced by managers today, but not one in which much progress has been made in the last decade or so.

9   Finding the Golden Fleece on the road ahead

The argument that reverberates throughout this chapter is that the transformational marketplace, which is developing around the world, demands new approaches and new methodologies for brand marketing and communication. Nowhere is that more evident than in the areas of brand budget development, allocation and measurement of returns. Thus, the growing belief that the focus must be much more on determining the proper identification on how much should be spent or invested and then how it can be properly allocated than has been done in the past. The old models of a percentage of past or future sales or profits or an estimate of how many units might be disposed of, pale in the face of the new empowered consumer who decides what to buy and when from an ever increasing range of products, services and suppliers. Truly, the future is in the planning, not the measurement.

9.1 Is media consumption the Golden Fleece?

In this chapter, a strong argument has been made for new approaches to budgeting and allocation of brand communication and marketing resources. The reasoning is simple: if better consumer-focused allocation is developed, better returns on investments should normally occur. Lousy allocation will result in lousy returns. It's that simple.

The approach outlined relies on media consumption measures, not something that is well developed either in the academic arena or in practice. Yet, consumption becomes the critical factor in a push and pull marketplace. Brand marketers can no longer rely on simple message distribution systems primarily because they do not account for what the consumer or customer or end user is doing. And, as the new media forms, particularly search, mobile and the social networks, become ever more pervasive, methods and approaches must be found to enable the marketer to know what messages consumers are receiving, what they are accessing and what is brand communication is occurring among and between them. Those 'customer conversations' are really what will drive brand success in the future.

9.2 Synergy – the mysterious ingredient

Given the rapid development of new media and communication forms and the consumer's increasing capability to access and use those new communication systems, the synergy among and between them becomes a critical variable. Where individual media forms, that is, television or newspapers or in-store commonly aggregated large number of people who could be accessed by the brand organization, the systems now in place made a great deal of sense. With the explosion of new media forms, the rapidly developing ability of consumers to capture, store, manipulate and use the information and materials they acquire, the understanding of how and in what way consumers acquire, combine and then use the various media alternatives become a critical variable in understanding how brands can and must communicate.

Quite honestly, very little is known about media synergy or whether or not one media form reinforces another or detracts from the overall effect. Part of the reason for this is the Western view of separation and individualization that permeates the culture. Eastern cultures are much more focused on holistic views of the marketplace and the systems which drive them. As consumers increasingly engage in media multitasking and simultaneous media consumption, synergy becomes the major predictive force in brand marketing and communication. Does one and one actually equal three or does one and one equal one and one-half? At this point, we simply don't know. We do know that consumers will increasingly make use of the brand communication forms available to them. They will make decisions based on what they experience and what they know. Brand marketers simply must move toward a more integrated and aligned use of the resources. If not, brands will become irrelevant and then, brand measurement will be irrelevant as well.

9.3   What happens next?

Given all the changes that have occurred and those still to come, the only thing a brand marketer can be sure of is that tomorrow won't be like today and it certainly won't be like yesterday. The transformational marketplace is here. We're experiencing some of the initial waves of change. More are sure to come.

What we can be sure of though is, it will be exciting and for those brand marketers who focus on the consumer and the customer, it likely will be a great deal of fun as well.

Appendix A: The 31 media alternatives measured in the SIMM studies

- Web site
- Word-of-mouth
- Television
- Cable
- Internet service provider (ISP)
- Broadband
- IPTV
- Search engine use
- Retail channel shopped
- Radio
- Article about product in media
- In-store promotion
- Newspapers
- Newspaper inserts
- Direct mail
- Magazine
- Internet advertising
- Outdoor billboards
- Picture phone
- Instant messenger
- E-mail advertising
- Yellow pages
- Satellite radio
- Text message
- MP3 player
- Web radio
- Video games

- Personal digital assistant (PDA)
- Cell phone
- Blogging
- TiVo

References

Aaker, D.A. (1991) *Managing Brand Equity*. New York: Free Press.

Colley, R. (1961) *Defining Goals for Measured Advertising Results*. New York: Association of National Advertisers.

Lavidge, R.J. and Steiner, G.A. (1961) 'A model for predictive measurements of advertising effectiveness', *The Journal of Marketing*, Vol. 25, No. 6, October, 59–62.

Schultz, D.E. and Pilotta, J.J. (2004) 'Developing the foundation for a new approach to understanding how media advertising works', paper presented at ESOMAR WAM Conference, Geneva, Switzerland.

Schultz, D.E., Pilotta, J.J. and Block, M.P. (2005) 'Implementing a media consumption model', paper presented at ESOMAR WAM Conference, Montreal, Canada.

Schultz, D.E., Pilotta, J.J. and Block, M.P. (2006) 'Media consumption and purchasing', paper presented at ESOMAR M3 Conference, Shanghai, China.

4
Marketing Mix Modelling and Return on Investment

Peter M. Cain

1 Introduction

The marketing mix model is a widely used tool to evaluate Return on Investment (ROI) and inform optimal allocation of the marketing budget. Economics and econometrics lie at the heart of the process. In the first place, the model structure is derived from microeconomic theories of consumer demand ranging from single equations of product sales to full interactive systems of brand choice. Secondly, econometric techniques are used to estimate demand response to marketing investments, separating product sales into base and incremental volume. Base sales represent the long-run or trend component of the product time series, driven by factors ranging from regular shelf price and selling distribution to underlying consumer brand preferences. Incremental volume, on the other hand, is essentially short-run in nature, capturing the week-to-week sales variation driven by temporary selling price, multi-buy promotions and above the line media activity. These are converted into incremental revenues or profits and benchmarked against costs to calculate ROI to each element of the marketing mix.

Focusing solely on incremental volumes in this way implies that conventional marketing mix models provide insight into short-term ROI only. As such, they often lead to marketing budget allocations biased towards promotional activity: short-run sales respond well to promotions, yet are less responsive to media activity – particularly for established brands. This, however, ignores the longer-term perspective: that is, the potential brand-building effects of successful media

94

campaigns on the one hand and the brand-eroding impacts of heavy price discounts on the other. Acknowledging and quantifying these features is crucial to a complete ROI evaluation and a more strategic budget allocation.

Measuring the long-run impact of marketing investments requires a focus on the base sales component of the marketing mix model. This is simply because any long-term brand-building effects reside in the level or trend component of the sales series and impact the evolution in base sales over time. The ability to uncover these effects depends crucially on the data and choice of econometric methodology used. The conventional approach uses static Ordinary Least Squares (OLS) techniques which impose a fixed or deterministic baseline. Not only can this give an artificial split into base and incremental volumes, it precludes any analysis of the long-run impact of marketing activity by construction. One solution is to apply the dynamic cointegrating Vector Autoregression (VAR) model, an estimation technique commonly used in the econometrics literature for evaluating the long-term effects of economic indicators. Examples in the marketing literature can be found in *inter alia* Dekimpe and Hanssens (1999). In practice, however, this technique is often impractical in the context of fully specified mix models. A preferable approach is to use a methodology that can directly separate both the short- and long-run features of the data – allowing a complete analysis of both in distinct stages. Time series regression analysis is a logical choice for two reasons. Firstly, all marketing mix models involve time-ordered data and are essentially time series equations with additional marketing mix components. Secondly, the technique provides a direct decomposition of any time-ordered data series into a trend, seasonal and random error component. It is then a natural step to decomposition of product sales into short-term marketing factors (incremental) and long-term base (trend). This generates an evolving baseline, which can then be meaningfully analysed to quantify long-run ROI.

In this chapter, we develop these issues in detail. Section 2 outlines the foundations of the marketing mix model. Against the background of the conventional approach, we put forward alternative theoretical and econometric frameworks for improved short-term ROI evaluation. The section is then completed with a technique for evaluating the long-term effects of marketing investments and how these may be combined with short-term results to provide total ROI. Section 3 discusses the managerial benefits of the mix model and the total returns on marketing. Section 4 concludes.

2   The modelling process

Evaluating total marketing ROI proceeds in five key stages as illustrated in Figure 4.1, ranging from the underlying economic model and level of analysis through to a complete evaluation of the long-term impact of marketing investments on sales and profits.

Steps 1–4 represent the key ingredients of short-term marketing ROI evaluation. Together, they comprise the basic framework of the standard marketing mix model. Two points are worthy of note here. Firstly, conventional approaches tend to overlook the microeconomic consumer demand structures underlying the model form. However, it is important to be aware of these so the best model(s) can be chosen for any particular situation. Secondly, econometric estimation of the model parameters tends to follow a standard OLS regression route – with little attention paid to the fundamental time series nature of the data involved. This is unfortunate, as considerable

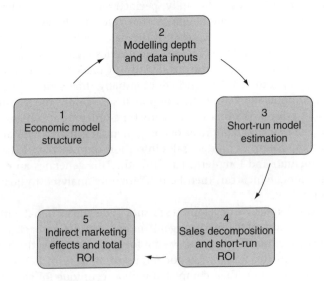

Figure 4.1   The marketing ROI modelling process

information can be lost leading to inaccurate short-term ROI measurement. Time series estimation techniques that accurately model both the short- and long-run components of the data are preferable. Step 5 completes the process, outlining an approach to long-run ROI measurement where consumer tracking research is merged with outputs from the short-term marketing mix model.

2.1 Economic model structure

All marketing mix models are based on microeconomic models of product demand with a view to inferring consumer response to each element of the marketing mix. Consequently, an important starting point is the type of consumer demand model used. Figure 4.2 presents a stylised structure of a product hierarchy designed to illustrate the various options available.

Each level in Figure 4.2 corresponds to a specific model of consumer demand at different degrees of product aggregation. Level 1 comprises single equation models run at individual product level, or aggregated into similarly priced and promoted groups or 'items'.

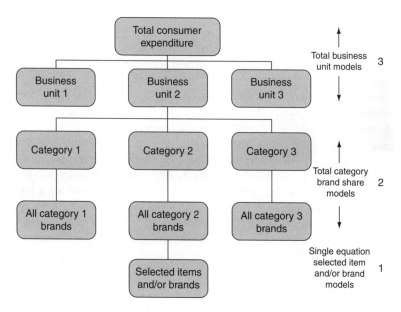

Figure 4.2   A modelling hierarchy of products, brands and business units

If the aim is to gain a picture of total brand performance, sets of single equations at product or item level can be estimated. Alternatively, the data can be aggregated into variants or a single brand variable. To gain a coherent picture of total category demand, on the other hand, we proceed to Level 2 models. Similarly, these too may comprise sets of product level equations. However, the number of required equations is often prohibitive. Consequently, products are generally aggregated to items, variants or total brand level. As we move to Level 3, models of total business units usually involve highly aggregated sales, marketing and macroeconomic data.

2.1.1   Single equation models

The conventional approach to modelling the marketing mix focuses on selected items and/or brands in the manufacturer's portfolio of products. This 'single-equation' approach generally uses the following type of demand model:

$$S_{it} = \exp\left(\alpha_i + T_i + \delta_i + \varepsilon_{it}\right) \prod_{j=1}^{n} \prod_{k=1}^{M} f_m(X_{kit})^{\beta_{ijk}} \tag{4.1}$$

Which stipulates that sales of product i (S_i) over time t are a multiplicative function (f_m) of a set of marketing and economic driver variables X_{kit}[1]. The demand equation is completed with an intercept α_i, trend (T_i), seasonal index (δ_i) and an error term ϵ_i. The intercept is equal to the mean of the sales data – net of the parameter weighted means of the explanatory variables – and equivalent to the expected level of non-marketed product sales. This is often referred to as *base* sales. The trend term caters for any observable 'drift' present in the base over time and the seasonal index caters for regular 'time-of-year' factors and period-specific holiday effects. The error term represents all unexplained factors influencing demand and must satisfy the usual properties of classical regression in order for us to interpret the demand parameters with confidence and precision. As it stands, equation (4.1) is non-linear. For the purposes of estimation, the model is converted into an additive form by taking natural logarithms thus:

$$LnS_{it} = \alpha_i + T_i + \delta_i + \sum_{j=1}^{n} \sum_{k=1}^{M} \beta_{ijk} \ln X_{kit} + \varepsilon_{it} \tag{4.2}$$

The log-linear single-equation level 1 approach is adequate if we wish to focus on single products at a time and is a popular choice due to the fact that estimated parameters β_{ijk} are immediately interpretable as demand elasticities. However, it does suffer from two key drawbacks.

Firstly, it is well known that the double logarithmic functional form is inconsistent with the adding up constraint of conventional microeconomic demand theory (Deaton and Muellbauer, 1980). Equation (4.2) is often applied in practice to several competing products in one group or 'category'. Each equation for product i is specified as a function of $k = 1 \ldots M$ of its own marketing mechanics together with $j = 1 \ldots n$ of the (competitive) marketing drivers of the other items in the group. Problems arise when the estimated volume steal from product i due to the marketing activity X_j of competitor products does not match total competitor volume gains. That is, it is perfectly possible that volume steal is either less than or greater than volume gains. Whereas this is usually interpreted as category growth or shrinkage respectively, it is simply a consequence of the fact that sets of single equations are unrelated to each other and do not 'add-up', telling us nothing about genuine category effects of product marketing.[2]

Secondly, marketing incremental is a gross figure: that is, each model delivers a total amount of incremental volume to each element of the marketing mix. However, we cannot accurately define the source of this incremental: specifically, how much is due to substitution from other brands and how much is due to category expansion effects?[3]

2.1.2   Total category models

To overcome these problems, simultaneous equation demand system approaches are required. There are several theoretical structures that can be used. On the one hand, we have continuous choice models such as Stone's Linear Expenditure system (Stone, 1954), the Rotterdam model (Theil, 1965; Barten, 1966) and the Almost Ideal Demand System (AIDS) of Deaton and Muellbauer (1980).[4] On the other hand, there are discrete choice approaches such as the attraction models illustrated in Nakanishi et al. (1974). Here we focus on the attraction model due to its more widespread use in the marketing literature. The functional form of the model is based on the notion that attractiveness of product i in a chosen category is a function of k marketing efforts X_k. This gives:

$$A_i = \exp\left(\alpha_i + T_i + \delta_i + \varepsilon_i\right) \prod_{j=1}^{n} \prod_{k=1}^{M} f_m(X_{kit})^{\beta_{ijk}} \qquad (4.3)$$

The volume share of product i as a proportion of total category volume sales is then defined as equal to its share of attractiveness out of total attraction of the category. Thus we have:

$$s_i = \frac{A_i}{\sum_{j=1}^{n} A_j} \qquad (4.4)$$

where A_i represents the attractiveness of brand i and $\sum_{j=1}^{n} A_j$ represents the total attractiveness of the category summed over all n brands. Substituting equation (4.3) into equation (4.4) gives us the general form of the sum-constrained market share model where all product shares sum to unity. As for the single equation approach, the resultant model form is non-linear and must be transformed in order to provide an estimable functional form. Taking logarithms of both sides of equation (4.4) and subtracting the pth product share in the system we have:

$$\ln(s_i) - \ln(s_p) = \ln(A_i) - \ln(A_p) \qquad (4.5)$$

Substituting equation (4.3) into equation (4.5) gives:

$$\ln\left[\frac{s_{it}}{s_{pt}}\right] = [\alpha_i - \alpha_p] + [T_i - T_p] + [\delta_i - \delta_p]$$

$$+ \sum_{k=1}^{M} \sum_{j=1}^{n} (\beta_{kij} - \beta_{kpj}) \ln X_{kjt} + [\varepsilon_i - \varepsilon_p] \qquad (4.6)$$

Equation (4.6) gives the general form of the sum-constrained log-ratio demand system, which predicts the (aggregated) probability of product choice from a consumer consideration set in terms of given marketing driver variables.[5] The model can be written as a set of *n-1* reduced form log-ratio share equations, each as a function of product-specific marketing effects β_{kij} for each marketing mix variable and a full set of direct competitor cross effects β_{kpj}.[6] The pth numeraire share equation is defined by the model adding up constraint – which is used to derive the underlying (structural) parameters of all n shares.

Data limitations and collinearity issues usually preclude estimation of model (Equation 4.6) as it stands. It is more usual to consider restricted versions of the model nested within this general extended form. Firstly, the *differential* effects model constrains all direct cross effects β_{kij} to zero – but allows product-specific marketing effects β_{kpj}. Secondly, the *constant effects* model goes further and imposes equal response effects β_k for all competing products. Both models can be seen as sets of cross equation parameter restrictions on the general model. Any combination of data admissible restrictions is feasible – leading to combinations of constant and differential effects model.[7]

Finally, since the specification of the attraction model is in log-ratio share form, we need to ensure that the marketing response estimates are invariant to the choice of pth numeraire share. Furthermore, the system requires a model for total category volume such that we can derive equations for product volume. The former is ensured by maximum likelihood estimation of the system.[8] The latter is dealt with by a category volume equation such as:

$$\ln CV_t = \alpha + T_i + \delta_t + \sum_{j=1}^{n}\sum_{k=1}^{K} \rho_{ij} \ln X_{kj} + \sum_{L=1}^{l} \phi_i Z_t + u_t \qquad (4.7)$$

Equation (4.7) is estimated in terms of relevant brand marketing variables X_{jt}, a range of macroeconomic drivers Z_t, trend and seasonal components. Together system (4.6) and equation (4.7) give a set of product volume equations which deal with both of the problems raised in the single-equation approach. Substitution effects and share elasticities are derived through the share model, and the impact of product-specific marketing effects on the category is estimated through the category model.[9]

2.1.3 Business unit models

It is rare for manufacturers to operate in just one category. The manufacturing portfolio generally comprises broad ranges of products across different categories known as business units. For example, categories such as detergents, soaps, deodorants, oral and skin care may be grouped under a wider business unit label such as Health and Personal Care. A 'bottom up' picture of total business unit marketing effectiveness may be obtained by aggregating results for all relevant manufacturer brands across a range of modelled categories. However, this generally requires a considerable number of models. An alternative 'top down' approach is to run models directly at a business unit level, with data aggregated across each manufacturer's portfolio of categories. A useful economic model at this highly aggregated level is the AIDS model of Deaton and Muellbauer (1980) illustrated in equations (4.8) and (4.9).

$$S_{BUit} = \alpha_i + T_i + \sigma_i + \sum_{j=1}^{n} \gamma_{ij} \ln p_{jt} + \sum_{m=1}^{M} \sum_{j=1}^{n} \phi_{mij} X_{mt} + \beta_i \ln \left[\frac{TCE_t}{\tilde{p}_t} \right] + \varepsilon_{it}$$

(4.8)

$$LnTCE_t = \alpha + T + \delta_i + \sum_{j=1}^{L} \phi_i Z_{lt} + u_t$$

(4.9)

Equation (4.8) indicates that the revenue share of total business unit sales for manufacturer i out of total consumers' expenditure (TCE) on categories across all manufacturers playing in the same business unit is a function of an index of aggregate prices and marketing variables (X_m), together with trend, seasonal index and deflated total consumers' expenditure.[10] Equation (4.9) specifies that TCE itself is a function of a range of macroeconomic variables Z_t. Together, equations (4.8) and (4.9) make up a joint model of aggregate consumer demand for each manufacturer's business unit, where shifts in overall macroeconomic activity, and their impact on business unit performance, feed naturally from (4.9) to (4.8).

The three levels of market mix modelling illustrated in this section highlight two key issues: namely, the microeconomic origins of alternative types of model on the one hand and how ROI analysis can be pitched at varying degrees of product aggregation on the other. It is important to recognise, however, that each model structure is not limited to each level of aggregation. For example, single equation volume models can be applied at any level of the hierarchy – they just lack the microeconomic consistency of the demand system

structures. Demand system approaches may also be used for competing groups of individual product lines, but require many component
equations to arrive at a full category scope. Combinations of both
are also possible, providing an integrated model of the manufacturer
portfolio. For example, demand system models can be used to gain a
complete picture of the total category at brand level. Single equation
approaches can then be used to drill down into the product detail
contained in each brand aggregate. In sum, a wide variety of options
are possible, with the types and combinations of models used tailored
to relevant business issues.

2.2   Modelling depth and data inputs

The economic models of Section 2.1 can be applied, in principle,
across a range of industries, as diverse as Fast Moving Consumer
Good (FMCG) to financial and automotive. In practice, however,
model choice is heavily dependent on available data and relevant
business issues. For example, full category data are often unavailable
to individual players in sectors such as financial services, thus leaving conventional single equation modelling as the only option. On
the other hand, such data are generally available in the Fast Moving Consumer Good (FMCG) or automotive sectors, thus allowing
applications of simultaneous equation category modelling. Once the
scope of available data has been determined and the relevant economic models identified, the next step is to specify the modelling
'depth' and driver variables involved.

2.2.1   Modelling depth

Product sales at each level of the hierarchy in Figure 4.2 constitute
'revealed' consumer demand for the product aggregate in question.
Models at each level may also be run at differing levels of aggregation
across the consumer as illustrated in Figure 4.3.

 The left-hand-side axis represents the sales metric over time at the
chosen level of the modelling hierarchy outlined in Section 2.1. The
bottom axis represents the sales channel or level of consumer aggregation: households, stores, groups of stores (chains or key accounts)
up to total market level. The right-hand-side axis indicates how these
groups may also be split by geographical region. Each block thus
depicts a time series for each regional-channel combination, designed
to demonstrate how the models of Section 2.1 can be estimated across

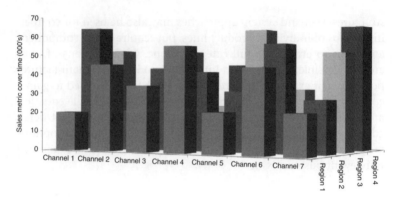

Figure 4.3   Levels of consumer aggregation

different cross-sectional units – where increased parameter precision can be gained from pooling time-based observations across different dimensions. Such models use longitudinal panel data sets and are known as Time Series Cross Section (TSCS) models. Household level panel models represent the lowest level of consumer aggregation and tend to reside solely in the academic domain, with many examples in the literature (*inter alia* Jedidi et al., 1999). Moving up the aggregation tree takes us first to store and then to key account panel models across regions and/or market level. Such models are readily offered on a commercial basis. Pure time-series-based models, involving single time series at market level, represent the highest level of consumer aggregation and often offered where limited cross-sectional data are available.

2.2.2   Demand drivers

Demand driver variables are chosen to represent the full marketing mix, ranging from selling distribution, price promotion, multibuy and display activity through to TV, press, magazine, radio and Internet investments. Media data are also often split up into separate campaigns to isolate differential effectiveness by message. Diminishing returns for increasing media weight are implicitly incorporated into the multiplicative form of equation (4.1). However, this is often augmented to incorporate non-constant elasticities to test for additional saturation effects. External drivers such as macroeconomic data on consumers' income, GDP and interest rates can also be used and generally sourced from government statistical departments. However, their use will depend on the level of product aggregation used. The minimum level at which such data will appear is in Level 1 models using highly aggregated sales metrics, Level 2 category models such as equation (4.7) or Level 3 models such as equation (4.9). It is highly unlikely that such data will feature as significant drivers in models for individual products at Level 1.

2.3 Short-run model estimation

The next step in the process is quantification of the sales response to variation in each of the marketing mix investments. This is where econometrics enters the picture: a statistical regression-based procedure to estimate the parameters of the theoretical demand functions outlined in Section 2.1, at the appropriate depth outlined in Section 2.2. It is important to recognise, however, that such demand functions, as they stand, are inadequate for estimation purposes. Firstly, they depict contemporaneous relationships between sales and marketing variables: this is as far as economic theory will take us in deriving an estimating form for the marketing mix model, but tells us nothing about the dynamics of sales adjustment to changes in the marketing mix. Consequently, it is implicitly assumed that consumers adjust immediately to changes in the driver variable(s). Secondly, underlying brand tastes are not modelled in any way. A time trend is often added to the intercept of the static functional forms of Section 2.1 to allow for a general drift in tastes over time, but this is purely deterministic and user-imposed. It tells us nothing about genuine long-term evolution in the sales data.

Both of these issues indicate that more flexible dynamic forms of the mix model are required for estimation purposes. This section focuses on two complementary specifications: autoregressive distributed lag (ADL) models and time varying parameter (TVP) models. ADL models improve the underlying *behavioural* relationship between sales and marketing by explicitly recognising that consumers take time to fully adjust to changes in marketing investments – due to factors such as brand loyalty, habit formation and short- to medium-term repeat purchase. TVP models, on the other hand, address the underlying *time series* properties of the sales series, recognising that sales also adjust to longer-run factors such as changes in brand tastes, potentially driven by a host of factors in which marketing may or may not play a role.

2.3.1   *ADL models*

A general dynamic functional form rewrites the static model as an Autoregressive Distributed Lag (ADL) function in terms of lagged sales together with current and past driver values. In the case of the single equation model (4.2), we have:

$$LnS_{it} = \alpha_i + T_i + \delta_i + \sum_{j=1}^{n}\sum_{k=1}^{M}\sum_{l=1}^{T}\beta_{ijk}\ln X_{kit-l} + \sum_{l=1}^{T}\lambda \ln S_{it-l} + \varepsilon_{it} \qquad (4.10)$$

This is known as a dynamic relationship and is intended to capture the short- to medium-term effects of marketing investments as consumers adjust to new levels of the relevant driver(s). Analogous specifications can also be applied to demand system approaches. However, the presence and final lag length (l) of the X_k and sales variables is purely data driven: *a priori* economic theory does not tell us precisely how consumers adjust. Nevertheless, many hypothesised forms of adjustment are nested within this general functional form, which dictate the ultimate shape of the adjustment path. This section considers three such models.

2.3.1.1   *Adstock.*   The Adstock concept was introduced into the marketing literature by Broadbent (1979) and represents the conventional approach to incorporating dynamics into the marketing mix model – applied solely to TV advertising. The idea is intended to capture the *direct* current and future effects of advertising, where a portion of the full effect is felt beyond the period of execution due to the interplay between media retention and the product purchase cycle. This is equivalent to a restricted form of the distributed lag model – nested in equation (4.10) – with lags (l) applied solely to the advertising (TVR) variable:

$$LnS_{it} = \alpha_i + T_i + \delta_i + \sum_{l=0}^{T}\beta_{l+1}\ln(TVR_{t-l}) + \sum_{j=1}^{n}\sum_{k=2}^{M}\beta_{ijk}\ln X_{kit} + \varepsilon_{it} \qquad (4.11)$$

Assuming that the distributed lag coefficients decline geometrically, we may write:

$$LnS_{it} = \alpha_i + T_i + \delta_i + \beta(1-\gamma)\sum_{l=0}^{T}\gamma^l \ln(TVR_{t-l}) + \sum_{j=1}^{n}\sum_{k=2}^{M}\beta_{ijk}\ln X_{kit} + \varepsilon_{it}$$

(4.12)

The parameter γ represents the appropriate retention rate, the value of which is bounded between 0 and 1, usually chosen via a search procedure to maximise the in-sample fit of the model: longer retention rates are indicative of a higher quality of advertising and/or a shorter consumer purchase cycle. This approach represents a concise way of encapsulating a distributed lag effect in one simple variable. Equation (4.12) represents the basic functional form of the bulk of marketing mix analyses, with demand parameters estimated using OLS regression techniques on panel or market level time series data.[11]

2.3.1.2 Partial adjustment. An alternative dynamic specification assumes that consumers partially adjust towards a desired or equilibrium sales level following a change in the marketing variables. This theory gives the following functional form:

$$LnS_{it} = \alpha_i^* + T_i^* + \delta_i^* + \sum_{j=1}^{n}\sum_{k=1}^{M}\beta_{ijk}^*\ln X_{kit} + \lambda^*\ln S_{t-1} + \varepsilon_{it}$$

(4.13)

where the parameter λ^* measures the rate of adjustment towards equilibrium.[12] As for the Adstock model, this is simply a restricted form of the full ADL specification. However, an implicit lag structure now appears via the lagged sales term. Consequently, the dynamic interpretation is different. Forms like (4.13) are often used to model direct current period marketing effects, where dynamic 'carryover' effects work *indirectly* through repeat purchase based on product performance.[13]

2.3.1.3 Error correction. An alternative re-writing of the ADL model (4.10) is in error correction form. For example a one-period lag with one explanatory variable X_k may be written as:

$$\Delta S_{it} = \alpha_i + T_i + \delta_i + \beta_1 \Delta X_{kt} - (1-\lambda)\left[S_{it-1} - \tilde{\beta}X_{kt-1}\right] + \varepsilon_{it}$$

(4.14)

which expresses the change in sales in terms of the change in X_k and the lagged levels of sales and X_k. Forms like (4.14) go one step further than (4.13). Rather than simply positing the existence of a desired level of product demand, the model hypothesises that an equilibrium relationship exists between the levels of X_k and sales. For example, suppose that the manufacturer strategy is to maintain a certain ratio between sales and TV advertising expenditure – a ratio determined by the parameter. An increase (decrease) in the level of advertising activity shifts the sales–TV relationship away from its strategic long-term ratio: that is, sales and advertising are knocked out of 'equilibrium'. Sales first increase (decrease) immediately by a factor β_1, followed by a further feedback increase (decrease) in sales to restore the underlying ratio. Analogously to equation (4.13), the rate of adjustment towards the equilibrium ratio is determined by the parameter $(1-\lambda)$. In this way equation (4.14) captures both the short-run per period changes in sales due to advertising together with the medium-term adjustment in sales over subsequent time periods as equilibrium is restored. A good example can be found in Baghestani (1991).

The most common dynamic specification used in marketing mix applications is the Adstock form (4.12), which is sometimes augmented with a lagged sales variable as in equation (4.13) to add a purchase feedback effect.[14,15] All such forms, however, retain the fixed intercept and trend component of model (4.2). Product demand is thus assumed to fluctuate around a constant level and deterministic drift factor (if present) and not permitted to adjust in line with evolving product tastes over time. With no allowance for systematic variation in product tastes, the potential for persistent or long-term effects of marketing is, therefore, overlooked.[16]

There are two ways of addressing this. In the first place, one can simply test for an evolving taste component in the sales data using conventional unit root tests and apply non-stationary forms of the error correction model (4.14). The mix model would then be estimated in first differenced form using the cointegrating VAR approach to econometrics (Johansen, 1996; Juselius, 2006), potentially involving equilibrium relationships between sales and other evolving variables. However, this approach is complex and impractical in the context of fully specified models where many variables are involved. Furthermore, the autoregressive-based unit root tests of Dickey and Fuller (1981) have low power against a deterministic trend alternative and, by ignoring any moving average structure in the data, display poor statistical properties (Schwert, 1987).

A preferable and more practical alternative is to allow the underlying sales level to evolve as an explicit component of the mix model. This is the approach taken by Time Varying Parameter econometrics, allowing us to extract any evolutionary taste component directly from the sales data, accurately separating short- and long-run variation. The short-run component provides the basis of marketing ROI as in the standard mix model. The long-run component, on the other hand, allows us to assess the determinants of systematic long-term evolution in a second step.

2.3.2   TVP econometrics

Marketing mix models at any level of the hierarchy in Figure 4.2 involve time-ordered sales observations. Consequently, they are essentially time series regressions with additional marketing driver variables – and should be estimated as such. Time series regression analysis is a statistical technique that decomposes the behaviour of any time-ordered data series into a trend, seasonal and random error component. The trend component represents evolution in the level of the sales series and is crucial to a well-specified marketing mix model. In the conventional static or dynamic approach of equations (4.2) and (4.12), this is dealt with by the regression intercept plus a linear deterministic (negative or positive) growth factor. However, trends in sales or business data rarely behave in such a deterministic fashion. Many markets, ranging from Fast Moving Consumer Good (FMCG) to durables, exhibit trends which evolve and vary over time indicative of shifts in various factors ranging from regular price and selling distribution to brand perceptions.[17] To accommodate this, the basic regression models of Section 2.1 need to be re-cast in a more flexible time series form. Using the single equation model (4.2) as an example, the general form is as follows:

$$LnS_{it} = \mu_{it} + \delta_{it} + \sum_{j=1}^{n}\sum_{k=1}^{n} \beta_{ijk} \ln X_{kit} + \varepsilon_{it} \qquad (4.15)$$

$$\mu_{it} = \mu_{it-1} + \lambda_{it-1} + \eta_{it} \qquad (4.15(a))$$

$$\lambda_{it} = \lambda_{it-1} + \xi_{it} \qquad (4.15(b))$$

$$\delta_{it} = -\sum_{j=1}^{p-1} \delta_{it-j} + \kappa_{it} \qquad \text{(4.15(c))}$$

$$\beta_{ikt} = \beta_{ikt-1} + \upsilon_{it} \qquad \text{(4.15(d))}$$

Equation (4.15) replaces the intercept α_i in equation (4.2) with a time varying (stochastic) trend μ_{it}, comprising two components described by equations 4.15(a) and (b). This is known as the local linear trend model (Harvey, 1989). Specifically, equation 4.15(a) allows the underlying sales level to follow a random walk with a growth factor λ_i, analogous to the conventional trend term T_i. Equation (4.15b) allows λ_i itself to follow a random walk. The variables η_{it} and ξ_{it} represent two mutually uncorrelated normally distributed white-noise error vectors with zero means and covariance matrices $\sum_{\eta}^2$ and $\sum_{\xi}^2$. Several dynamic structures are encompassed within this general specification. For example, if both covariance matrices are non-zero, the level of product demand follows a random walk with stochastic drift. If $\sum_{\eta}^2 \neq 0$ and $\sum_{\xi}^2 = 0$, the drift component is deterministic. If $\sum_{\eta}^2 \neq 0$ and the growth factor is zero then the levels follow a random walk without drift. If both covariance matrices are zero, the data are trend stationary and the model collapses to a standard static OLS model with deterministic drift. In this way, the system can accommodate both stationary and non-stationary product demand allowing the data to decide between them. Equation 4.15(c) specifies seasonal effects, which are constrained to sum to zero over any one year to avoid confusion with other model components. Stochastic seasonality is allowed for using dummy variables, where p denotes the number of seasons per year, δt is the seasonal factor corresponding to time t and κ_{it} is a random error with mean 0 and covariance matrix δ_κ^2. If the latter is zero, then seasonality is deterministic. Finally, equation 4.15(d) allows the regression parameter for marketing variable k to evolve over the sample with a random error υ_{it} with mean 0 and covariance matrix δ_υ^2.

The dynamic time series formulation can be applied to models at all levels of the hierarchy in Figure 4.2 and provides a fully flexible framework for the market mix model with several key benefits. In the first place, product demand is directly decomposed into long-term and short-term components. Specifically, μ_{it} in equation 4.15(a) measures long-run changes in demand arising through shifts in underlying consumer tastes, leaving the β_{ijk} parameters of equation 4.15 to accurately measure short-run demand changes due to current period marketing activity. The result is a more realistic split into base and incremental volumes and more accurate short-term ROI calculation.

Secondly, the framework can accommodate the conventional behavioural dynamics outlined in Section 2.3.1. For example, advertising distributed lag effects can be incorporated in equation 4.15 in the form of a conventional Adstock variable as in equation (4.12). Improved short- and medium-term dynamic specification here provides a cleaner read on the long-term evolving component of the sales series.[18]

Thirdly, the framework naturally incorporates dynamic evolution in marketing response effects by adding additional time series equations for the response parameters β_{ij}. This is particularly important if we wish to test for shifts in marketing efficiencies over time – such as evolution in promotional and regular price elasticities for example.

Finally, having isolated the short-term impact of marketing, the extracted trend component μ_{it} allows us to build auxiliary models that focus specifically on the causes of longer-term adjustment. These can range from the impact of regular selling price, distribution and exogenous demand shocks, through to long-run effects of marketing activities. This step lies at the heart of total marketing ROI evaluation and is developed fully in Section 2.5.

2.4   Sales decomposition and short-run ROI

2.4.1   *Single equation approach*

Estimated marketing response parameters are generally used to decompose product sales into base and incremental volume. Base sales reflect the underlying trend in the data, indicative of long-run consumer product preferences. An application of the single equation time series model 4.15–4.15(d), with a distributed lag advertising variable covering two national TV media campaigns, is illustrated in Figure 4.4 depicting the sales pattern of an FMCG face-cleansing product. All short-term sales variation is clearly explained in terms of advertising, average price cuts, promotional and incremental selling distribution, features, competitive activity and seasonal demand. Base sales evolve slowly over the sample, settling from mid-2005 to mid-2006, increase until late 2006 and decline gently for the rest of

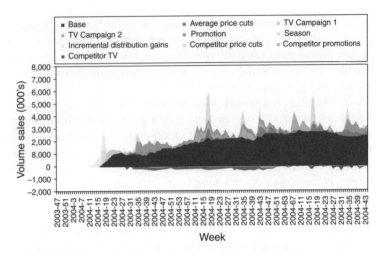

Figure 4.4   Sales decomposition with evolving baseline*
Source: Cain (2008).

the period. Total incremental volume is then used to calculate the percentage of sales volume explained by each of the sales drivers.

A large proportion of incremental sales volume is driven by TV advertising over the period – giving an average uplift of 6 per cent over base sales. Whereas this is reasonable for established brands in the industry – and consistent with decent cut through as measured by advertising awareness scores – the early heavyweight launch campaign delivers below average return for a new product in the market, bringing down the overall short-term TV ROI. Seasonal demand, the initial distribution drive and increases in in-store presence over the sample all contribute a significant percentage of incremental volume. Promotional activity, in the form of multi-buys, also play a significant role – yet pure price cuts drive little volume. Competitor losses – representing the potential sales volume the brand could have achieved had the competitors not engaged in those activities – amounts to an average of approximately 5 per cent of total sales volume over the sample – with the bulk of lost volume due to competitor TV media.

2.4.2   Category approach and the relative view

Decompositions of absolute sales volume are an important part of the process, but only tell part of the story. To provide additional

direction on marketing strategies, manufacturers often wish to know
whether reported incremental marketing effectiveness is good or bad
in the context of the overall category. To answer this question, a set
of benchmarks is needed. The usual approach is to appeal to historical studies of similar brands in the category. However, these are not
like-for-like comparisons since we are comparing studies at different
points in time, at different stages of the product lifecycle(s) and with
each study potentially subject to a whole host of different influencing factors. The category modelling approach outlined in Section 2.1,
on the other hand, provides a set of directly comparable benchmarks
over the same time period. These come in two stages.

The first stage provides an estimate of the overall net performance
of the brand's marketing strategy relative to all other brands in the
category. This is illustrated in Figure 4.5, where the model presented
in Figure 4.4 has been re-estimated as part of a category system of
equations using the dynamic category model analogue of equations
4.15–4.15(d).

Figure 4.5 gives the brand manager a bird's eye view of its net
marketing performance in the context of the whole category: values
above and below the horizontal axis are indicative of a performance
above and below the category average respectively. Here we can see

Figure 4.5 Relative brand marketing volume

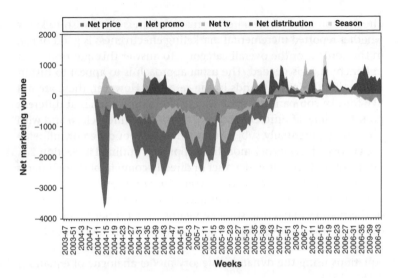

Figure 4.6   Drivers of relative brand marketing volume

that the client's brand marketing is underperforming for much of the sample. It is natural to want to know which element(s) of the marketing mix are driving this inefficiency.

The second stage answers this question by identifying the contribution of each individual marketing mechanic to the over- or under-performance of the overall marketing strategy. This is illustrated in Figure 4.6, which simply presents an alternative view of the model output to that in Figure 4.4. Each element of marketing volume for the client brand is now quantified relative to all other brands in the category.

Figure 4.6 provides valuable additional insights that are lost to standard single-equation studies of brand sales volume. Whereas absolute short-term TV media return is a reasonable 6 per cent uplift over base, in relative terms the client brand is losing volume due to its advertising strategy over a significant part of the sample (2004 week 40 through to 2005 week 33). This highlights a relatively weak media strategy – otherwise hidden if we concentrate on absolute volumes alone. A similar story emerges for selling distribution, where respectable absolute incremental volume gains hide a weak relative position – particularly during the launch drive. This helps to explain the poor absolute volume returns for the TV launch campaign. The poor average price position echoes the poor absolute price cut return evident in Figure 4.4: the brand's average price position in the category needs to be reviewed. The favourable promotional picture of Figure 4.4 is preserved in the relative view: the brand's promotional positioning is pitched correctly.

2.5 Indirect marketing effects and total ROI

Short-term ROI, whether viewed in absolute or relative form, is only part of the story. Marketing investments do more than simply drive incremental sales volumes. In the first place, successful TV campaigns serve to build trial, stimulate repeat purchase and maintain healthy consumer brand perceptions. In this way, advertising can drive and sustain the level of brand base sales.[19] Secondly, advertising can affect the degree of product price sensitivity – thereby enabling the brand to command higher price premia. Only by quantifying such indirect effects can we evaluate the true ROI to marketing investments and arrive at an optimal strategic balance between them.

Estimation of indirect effects requires four key data inputs: marketing investments, brand perceptions, base sales and price elasticity evolution. Base sales evolution indicates the extent to which new purchasers are converted into loyal consumers – through persistent repeat purchase behaviour and lasting shifts in consumer product tastes. This, in turn, can lead to shifts in price elasticity as stronger equity reduces demand sensitivity to price change. Brand perceptions are forged by product experience, driving product tastes and repeat purchase behaviour. Marketing investments, in turn, work directly on product perceptions. This reasoning creates the flow illustrated in Figure 4.7, where marketing investments are linked to variation in base sales and price elasticity via brand perception data. Given the evolutionary nature of the base sales (and other) data involved, the appropriate estimation process follows the five key stages outlined in Sections 2.5.1–2.5.5.[20]

2.5.1 *Estimating evolution in base sales and price sensitivity*

Evolution in base sales and price sensitivity can be derived directly from the time series approach to the marketing mix model outlined in Section 2.3.2. For example, base sales from the face-cleansing product model presented in Section 2.4, together with estimated variation

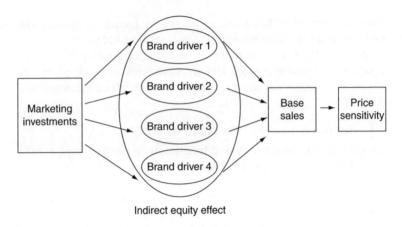

Figure 4.7 The indirect effects of marketing

in average price elasticity, are illustrated in Figure 4.8. Price sensitivity falls from −1.80 at the beginning of the sample to −1.30 at the beginning of 2006 – in line with a rising loyal consumer base after product launch. Price sensitivity rises thereafter to approximately −1.40 by the end of the sample.

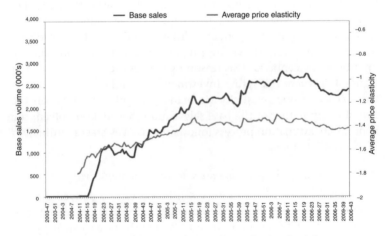

Figure 4.8 Time series evolution in bases sales and price elasticity

2.5.2   Identifying relevant consumer brand perceptions

Secondly, important consumer beliefs or attitudes towards the brand are identified. These will encompass statements about the product, perception of its value, quality and image. Such data are routinely supplied by primary consumer research tracking companies. Data are usually recorded weekly over time – often rolled up into four weekly moving average time series to minimise the influence of sampling error. An example is illustrated in Figure 4.9, which plots the evolving baseline of Figure 4.4 alongside advertising TVR investments and brand perception data relating to fragrance and perceived product value.[21]

2.5.3   Contribution of brand perceptions to brand demand and price sensitivity

Thirdly, we establish the impact of relevant tracking measures on brand demand and price sensitivity. Brand image tracking data represent the variation in consumer brand perceptions over time. Extracted base sales represent evolution of observed brand purchases or long-run brand demand – driven by trends in shelf price, selling

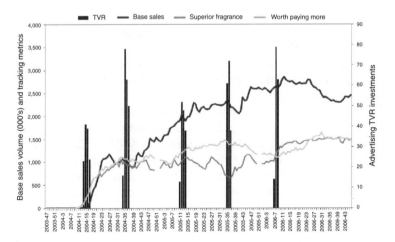

Figure 4.9   Evolution of base and consumer tracking statements*
Source: Cain (2008).

distribution and, crucially, brand perceptions.[22] Regression analysis is used to identify relationships between these variables. When evolving variables are involved, we must be careful to avoid spurious correlations where the analysis is simply picking up unrelated trending activity. Only then can we interpret the regression coefficients as valid estimates of the importance of each of the base demand drivers. The cointegrated VAR model (Johansen, 1996; Juselius, 2006) is used for this purpose and demonstrated with the following model structure.

$$
\begin{bmatrix} \Delta X_{1t} \\ \Delta X_{2t} \\ \Delta X_{3t} \\ \Delta X_{4t} \\ \Delta X_{5t} \\ \Delta X_{6t} \\ \Delta X_{7t} \end{bmatrix} = \begin{bmatrix} \pi_{11} \pi_{12} \pi_{13} \pi_{14} \pi_{15} \pi_{16} \pi_{17} \\ \pi_{21} \pi_{22} \pi_{23} \pi_{24} \pi_{25} \pi_{26} \pi_{27} \\ \pi_{31} \pi_{32} \pi_{33} \pi_{34} \pi_{35} \pi_{36} \pi_{37} \\ \pi_{41} \pi_{42} \pi_{43} \pi_{44} \pi_{45} \pi_{46} \pi_{47} \\ \pi_{51} \pi_{52} \pi_{53} \pi_{54} \pi_{55} \pi_{56} \pi_{57} \\ \pi_{61} \pi_{62} \pi_{63} \pi_{64} \pi_{65} \pi_{66} \pi_{67} \\ \pi_{71} \pi_{72} \pi_{73} \pi_{74} \pi_{75} \pi_{76} \pi_{77} \end{bmatrix} \begin{bmatrix} X_{1t-1} \\ X_{2t-1} \\ X_{3t-1} \\ X_{4t-1} \\ X_{5t-1} \\ X_{6t-1} \\ X_{7t-1} \end{bmatrix} + \begin{bmatrix} \varepsilon_{1t} \\ \varepsilon_{2t} \\ \varepsilon_{3t} \\ \varepsilon_{4t} \\ \varepsilon_{5t} \\ \varepsilon_{6t} \\ \varepsilon_{7t} \end{bmatrix} \qquad (4.16)
$$

Equation (4.16) represents an unrestricted VAR model, the multivariate analogue of equation (4.13), re-parameterised as a Vector Error Correction Model (VECM), the multivariate analogue of equation (4.14).[23] Variables X_{1t}–X_{7t} represent base sales, average price elasticity evolution, regular shelf price, selling distribution, two image statements and advertising data.[24] Model (4.16) is first used to test for *equilibrium* relationships between the variables: that is, relationships which tend to be restored when disturbed such that the series follow long-run paths together over time. Conceptually, this occurs if linear combinations of the variables provide trendless (stationary) relationships, implying that the π matrix of equation (4.16) is of reduced rank and the variables cointegrate. With n trending I(1) variables, the π matrix may be up to rank $n-1$, with $n-1$ corresponding equilibrium relationships to be tested as part of the model process.[25] For ease of exposition – and since we are focusing primarily on the drivers of base sales and price sensitivity – we assume a rank of 2 and thus just two linearly independent cointegrating relationships. This allows us to factorise (4.16) as:

$$
\begin{bmatrix} \Delta X_{1t} \\ \Delta X_{2t} \\ \Delta X_{3t} \\ \Delta X_{4t} \\ \Delta X_{5t} \\ \Delta X_{6t} \\ \Delta X_{7t} \end{bmatrix} = \begin{bmatrix} \alpha_{11}\,\alpha_{12}\,\alpha_{13} \\ \alpha_{21}\,\alpha_{22}\,\alpha_{23} \\ \alpha_{31}\,\alpha_{32}\,\alpha_{33} \\ \alpha_{41}\,\alpha_{42}\,\alpha_{43} \\ \alpha_{51}\,\alpha_{52}\,\alpha_{53} \\ \alpha_{61}\,\alpha_{62}\,\alpha_{63} \\ \alpha_{71}\,\alpha_{72}\,\alpha_{73} \end{bmatrix} \begin{bmatrix} \beta_{11} & 0 & \beta_{31} & \beta_{41} & \beta_{51} & \beta_{61} & 0 \\ \beta_{12} & \beta_{22} & 0 & 0 & \beta_{52} & \beta_{62} & 0 \\ 0 & 0 & 0 & 0 & 0 & 0 & \beta_{73} \end{bmatrix} \begin{bmatrix} X_{1t-1} \\ X_{2t-1} \\ X_{3t-1} \\ X_{4t-1} \\ X_{5t-1} \\ X_{6t-1} \\ X_{7t-1} \end{bmatrix} + \begin{bmatrix} \varepsilon_{1t} \\ \varepsilon_{2t} \\ \varepsilon_{3t} \\ \varepsilon_{4t} \\ \varepsilon_{5t} \\ \varepsilon_{6t} \\ \varepsilon_{7t} \end{bmatrix}
$$

$$(4.16a)$$

Equation 4.16(a) represents a cointegrated VAR representation of the system – with each first differenced equation driven by (stationary) advertising investments and two cointegrating or equilibrium relationships between base sales, average price elasticity, regular price evolution, selling distribution and the two image statements. The parameters β_{11}–β_{61} and β_{12}–β_{62} represent the cointegrating parameters. If we take the first cointegrating vector, and normalise on base sales (X_1) by setting β_{11} to unity, then β_{31}, β_{41} β_{51} and β_{61} represent the impact of the regular price level, selling distribution and the two image statements on base sales.[26] If we then take the second cointegrating vector and normalise on price elasticity (X_2) by setting β_{22} to unity, then β_{12}, β_{52} and β_{62} represent the impact of base sales and the two image statements on price sensitivity. Additional identifying constraints can be placed on the vectors. For example, we would expect base sales evolution to drive average price sensitivity – as per the flow illustrated in Figure 4.7 – but not vice versa. Thus we would set β_{21} to zero in the first cointegrating relationship. Furthermore, unless we have reason to believe that the level of regular price and selling distribution influences average price sensitivity, we would set β_{32} and β_{42} to zero in the second cointegrating vector.

Normalisation restrictions are quite arbitrary – and reflect assumptions on which variables are adjusting in the system: that is, the endogenous variables and direction of causality. For example, by normalising on X_1 and X_2 in each of the cointegrating vectors, we pre-suppose that image statements drive base sales and price sensitivity. However, it may be that causality runs in the other, or both, directions. The significance of the parameters α_{11}, α_{51} and α_{61} in the equations for ΔX_1, ΔX_5 and ΔX_6 provide the relevant information for base sales. Suppose α_{11} is negative and significant in the equation for ΔX_1, yet α_{51} and α_{61} are zero in equations ΔX_5 and ΔX_6. This tells us that base sales adjust (error correct) to shifts in image statements X_5 and X_6, at a rate α_{11} weighted by β_{51} and β_{61} respectively. However, image statements do not adjust to movements in base sales. Brand perceptions are (weakly) exogenous and *Granger* cause base sales (Granger, 1988). However, if α_{51} and α_{61} are positive and significant in equations for ΔX_5 and ΔX_6 then image statements do adjust to movements in base sales. Causality is bi-directional: from image to base and vice versa. Similar reasoning applies to the equation for ΔX_2, where, for a causal relationship from image statements to price sensitivity, we would expect α_{22} to be negative and significant with α_{52} and α_{62} equal to zero in the equations for ΔX_5 and ΔX_6. A negative and significant estimate of α_{12} would also tell us that base sales Granger cause price sensitivity.

2.5.4   Linking marketing investments to base sales

Finally, model 4.16(a) is used to estimate the full (long-term) impact of advertising on brand perceptions and the impact of the latter on base sales and price sensitivity. To do this, we make use of the Moving Average representation of the cointegrated VAR model 4.16(a) – written in matrix form as follows:

$$X_t = A + C \sum_{i=0}^{t} \varepsilon_i + \sum_{i=0}^{\infty} C_i^* \varepsilon_{t-i} \qquad (4.17)$$

Equation (4.17) shows that the model can be broken down into three components: initial starting values (A) for the variables, a non-stationary permanent component and a stationary component – represented by the cointegrating vectors themselves. The non-stationary C matrix – known as the Moving Average impact matrix – is illustrated in Figure 4.10 and provides the long-term impact of base sales on price sensitivity, image statements on base sales and advertising on image statements: each may then be combined to predict the net indirect impact of advertising on base sales and price sensitivity.

Each column of Figure (4.10) represents the cumulated empirical shocks to each equation of the VECM system 4.16(a).[27] Reading across in rows, the parameters indicate the long-term (permanent) impact of such cumulated shocks on the levels of the variables in the system. For example, the first row indicates that the long-term behaviour of

	ε_{x1}	ε_{x2}	ε_{x3}	ε_{x4}	ε_{x5}	ε_{x6}	ε_{x7}
X_1	C_{11}	C_{12}	C_{13}	C_{16}	$\boldsymbol{C_{15}}$	$\boldsymbol{C_{16}}$	0
X_2	$\boldsymbol{C_{21}}$	C_{22}	C_{23}	C_{24}	C_{25}	C_{26}	C_{27}
X_3	C_{31}	C_{32}	C_{33}	C_{34}	C_{35}	C_{36}	C_{37}
X_4	C_{41}	C_{42}	C_{43}	C_{44}	C_{45}	C_{46}	C_{47}
X_5	C_{51}	C_{52}	C_{53}	C_{54}	C_{55}	C_{56}	$\boldsymbol{C_{57}}$
X_6	C_{61}	C_{62}	C_{63}	C_{64}	C_{65}	C_{66}	$\boldsymbol{C_{67}}$
X_7	0	0	0	0	0	0	0

Figure 4.10   Moving average impact matrix

X_1 is determined by shocks in X_2–X_6 with weights C_{12}–C_{16}. Shocks in X_7 have no direct impact since base sales do not contain any of the direct impact of TV advertising by construction.[28] The final row is populated with zeros, indicating that shocks of all variables in the system have no long-term impact on advertising. This follows by construction since X_7 is a stationary variable.

For the permanent indirect impacts of advertising on base sales, the parameters of interest are C_{15}, C_{16}, C_{57} and C_{67}. The latter two parameters measure the impact of advertising shocks on image statements X_5 and X_6 respectively. Parameters C_{15} and C_{16} on the other hand measure the impact of shocks in image statements X_5 and X_6 on base sales. The net indirect impact of 1 per cent changes in advertising and both image statements on base sales is, therefore, $\%\{(C_{15}^* C_{57}) + (C_{16}^* C_{67})\}$. The impact of base sales on price sensitivity is given by parameter C_{21}. The impact of advertising on base sales is thus augmented with $\%C_{21}^*[\%\{(C_{15}^* C_{57}) + (C_{16}^* C_{67})\}]$ to incorporate the impact of advertising on price sensitivity.[29]

2.5.5   Calculating the full long-run impact

Estimated baseline impacts of marketing investments are part of the long-run sales trend and as such generate a stream of effects extending into the foreseeable future: positive for TV advertising and (potentially) negative for heavy promotional weight. These must be quantified if we wish to measure the full extent of such effects. To do so, we first note that in practice we would not expect future benefit streams to persist indefinitely into the future. Various factors dictate that such benefits will decay over time. Firstly, the value of each subsequent period's impact will diminish as loyal consumers eventually leave the category and/or switch to competing brands. Secondly, future benefits will be worth less as uncertainty increases. To capture these effects, we exploit a standard discounting method used in financial accounting which quantifies the current value of future revenue streams. The calculation used for each marketing investment is written as:

$$PV_i = \sum_{t=1}^{N} \frac{C_{i0}^* d_i^t}{(1+r)^t} \tag{4.18}$$

where PV_i denotes the Present Value of future indirect revenues accruing to marketing investment i, C_{i0} represents the indirect benefit calculated over the model sample, d represents the per period decay rate of subsequent indirect revenues over N periods and r represents a discount rate reflecting increasing uncertainty. The final PV of indirect marketing revenue streams will depend critically on the chosen values of d and r. The benefit decay rate can be chosen on the basis of established norms or estimated from historical data. The discount rate is chosen to reflect the product manufacturer's internal rate of return on capital: a higher discount rate reflects greater uncertainty around future revenue streams.

The indirect 'base-shifting' impact over the model sample, together with the decayed PV of future revenue streams, quantifies the long-run base impact of advertising and promotional investments. The value created by the impact of advertising on price elasticity, on the other hand, derives from the fact that the brand can now charge a higher price for the same quantity with less impact on marginal revenue. The reduced impact of price increases on revenues, weighted by the advertising contribution to price elasticity evolution, provides the additional value impact of advertising. Both the base and price elasticity revenue effects may then be combined with the weekly revenues calculated from the short-run modelling process. Benchmarking final net revenues against initial outlays then allows calculation of a more holistic ROI to marketing investments.[30]

3 Managerial benefits

The benefits and uses of the conventional marketing mix model are extensive. As a minimum, model results are used to provide ROI measurement and a purely retrospective view of marketing performance: that is, what worked and what didn't. This step may then be augmented in two key ways. In the first place, elasticity estimates can be used to advise on optimal allocation of the marketing budget. Secondly, marketing elasticities allow simulation of the likely consequences of alternative mix scenarios – both retrospectively and from a forward looking perspective if future marketing plans are available. This leads naturally onto the use of the model for short- to medium-term forecasting.

Re-formulating the conventional mix model to explicitly capture both short- and long-term sales variation takes us a step further. Not only does it provide a more accurate set of deliverables but lays the foundation of the long-run modelling processes outlined in Section 2. This, in turn, delivers two key commercial benefits.

(i) Enhanced strategic budget allocation

Budget allocation decisions based on the results of short-term mix model results are short-run focused by construction, often favouring heavy promotional activity over media investments. This often leads to a denigration of brand equity in favour of short-run revenue gain. Incorporating long-run returns, however, provides a more holistic balance reflecting strategic brand-building media activity.

(ii) Enhanced media creative building

A key part of the flow illustrated in Figure 4.7 is the equilibrium relationship between consumer brand perceptions, base sales and price elasticity. This relationship can be used to test for causal links between the data. Understanding which key brand characteristics drive brand demand and price elasticity in this way can help to clarify the media creative process for more effective long-term brand strategy.

Neither strategic benefit is possible if we rely on conventional market mix modelling alone, illustrating the additional insights that can be obtained from a combination of primary consumer research and modern time series analysis of secondary source sales and business data.

4   Conclusions

This chapter has sought to illustrate the complete structure of the marketing mix modelling process, ranging from the microeconomic consumer theory underlying alternative functional forms, dynamic estimating specifications through to models of long-term consumer behaviour. Throughout, three key issues have been demonstrated.

Firstly, all marketing mix models are rooted in economic theories of the consumer – and as such appropriate theoretical models need to be chosen for each market, category and business issue to hand. Practical applications of the mix model tend to routinely apply the standard single equation double logarithmic functional form regardless of circumstance. This is not necessarily the best route and superior models can be developed depending on the data available.

Secondly, dynamic form and estimation technique are crucial. Conventional dynamic marketing mix models only go so far and the estimation structures used are inadequate for modelling time series data, where it is imperative to correctly deal with the season and evolving trend or baseline inherent in most economic time series. A preferable and more flexible approach is to re-structure the mix model to explicitly model both the short and long-run features of the data.

Finally, not only does the time series structure provide more accurate short-run marketing results but, when combined with evolution in intermediate brand perception measures, allows for an evaluation of the long-run impact of marketing activities. This illustrates how intermediate brand perception data can be shown to (Granger) cause brand sales and, contrary to the concerns raised by Binet et al. (2007), used to improve long-term business performance.

Notes

1. Standard (additive) linear forms are also used. However, the multiplicative model is often chosen due to the implied relationships between demand and the chosen explanatory variables. For example, demand drops exponentially to zero as price approaches infinity and advertising exhibits diminishing returns as weight increases. These, together with

the implied synergies between the variables, are usually deemed desirable properties.

2. Violation of the adding up property refers to the fact that single-equation functional forms such as (4.2) give distorted expenditure patterns across the modelled products that are greater or less than total expenditure across the group.

3. This problem can be partly alleviated by specifying marketing effects in relative terms. For example, price in each demand equation can enter in absolute and relative terms providing an elasticity decomposition into two components: a relative demand response when price of good *i* changes relative to all other goods in the group and a matched demand response when prices of all products in the group move together. Although analogous to a separation of substitution and category level effects, this approach is still inconsistent with the adding up constraint.

4. See Cain (2005) for an application of the dynamic AIDS model.

5. The log-centred form of the attraction model is fully discussed in Nakanishi and Cooper (1974). The log-ratio approach used in the text provides equivalent parameter estimates and is easier to work with (see Houston et al., 1992).

6. Note that the parameter estimates of (4.9) are reduced form in that they are a composite of structural and residually defined parameter estimates of the pth product.

7. The Multiplicative Competitive Interaction (MCI) and Multi-Nomial-Logit (MNL) forms of the attraction model are based on a logic choice structure and derived from the consumer's utility function – where the relative odds of choosing product *i* over *j* is the same, no matter what other alternatives are available. This embodies the Independence of Irrelevant Alternatives (IIA) property which implies that substitution between products in response to marketing mix changes is in proportion to market share. This property is only true for the constant effects and differential model forms. Incorporating combinations of direct cross effects allows us to test deviations away from this basic competitive structure, where substitution may also be related to similarity of product characteristics.

8. Since each equation in system (4.6) contains the same set of explanatory variables, OLS regression estimation automatically satisfies adding up – and parameter estimates are invariant to choice of *numeraire*. As soon as we move to the constant or differential effects form, or combinations thereof, we are imposing cross-equation zero restrictions on the model structure leading to a non-diagonal error covariance matrix. Maximum likelihood estimation is then required to ensure invariance (Barten, 1969).

9. More flexible category expansion effects can be derived via inclusion of an outside good directly into the share system – with no need for a total category volume model. However, specification of the outside good is contingent on estimated potential market size and can be problematic.

10. Note that the dependent variable in this model is value share – as opposed to volume share in the category model structure of Section 2.1. This is a consequence of the alternative microeconomic foundations underlying the model. The functional form of the AIDS model is derived from the classic consumer utility maximisation problem: namely, the choice of optimal quantities of goods demanded subject to a fixed money income constraint. As such it is a continuous choice model since consumers demand optimal quantities of *all* goods in the system. This can be applied at many levels of aggregation but is best suited to highly aggregated data sets where it is natural to invoke the concept of the aggregate consumer.

11. The declining geometric lag restriction is just one possibility. Alternative (finite) lag structures may be imposed such as Polynomial Distributed lags (Almon, 1965), which allow tests of advertising 'wear-in', where maximum response to advertising can occur after the period of deployment.

12. Estimated parameter λ^* equals $(1-\phi)$, where the adjustment rate ϕ plays the same role as the retention rate γ in equation (4.12). The closer ϕ is to one, the more adjustment is immediate. As ϕ approaches zero, so consumers take longer to adjust and marketing impacts are 'stretched' over a longer time horizon.

13. An alternative approach is to apply an infinite distributed lag structure to the explanatory variable(s) in equation (4.2) and apply a Koyck transform (Koyck, 1954). This gives an observationally equivalent form to (4.13) with a moving average error term. Both the partial adjustment and Koyck forms have been extensively examined in the marketing literature (*inter alia* Clarke, 1976; Mela et al., 1997). Note, however, that the lagged sales term captures a general persistence applying common dynamics to all variables in the model. Consequently, it is not possible to isolate the differential dynamic effects due to each marketing mechanic.

14. This is somewhat *ad hoc* as it can be argued that one partially double-counts the other: that is, the Adstock form is a truncated form of the Koyck model – which itself is observationally equivalent to the purchase feedback model. Separating carryover and purchase reinforcement effects requires an alternative theoretical specification. See Givon and Horsky (1990).

15. The error correction model is rarely used in practice since the dynamics require relationships between continuous variables – as illustrated in Baghestani (1991). The level error correction term in (4.14) cannot incorporate the short- to medium-term dynamics of discrete variables such as advertising TVR data and temporary price cuts frequently used in marketing mix studies. Regular shelf price and selling distribution are generally the only conventional continuous regressor variables capable of forming error-correcting relationships with sales.

16. This essentially assumes that sales are stationary. Deterministic trends, such as in equation (4.10), impose an arbitrary view of taste evolution, where sales are essentially assumed to be trend stationary.

17. See Dekimpe and Hanssens (1995) for a survey.
18. Specifying the underlying demand level to evolve as a random walk essentially caters for situations where the explanatory variables cannot fully explain the level of sales. Since the random walk form contains elements at all frequencies, it can also reflect missing short- and medium-term information. For example, promotional lags measuring post-promotional dips will be reflected as downward shifts in μ_i.
19. Conversely, excessive price promotional activity can negatively influence base sales evolution – via denigrating brand perceptions and stemming repeat purchase.
20. Note that for any long-term or permanent indirect brand-building effects to exist, brand sales must be evolving. This is true if Model 2(a) encompasses the conventional mix model – with base sales representing the evolutionary component. The flow illustrated in Figure 4.7 is often referred to as a Path Model and estimated using Structural Equation Modelling (SEM) techniques. However, conventional SEM analysis is not suitable for evolving or non-stationary data in levels.
21. Selected brand image statements are often highly collinear. Consequently, preliminary *factoring* analysis is usually undertaken to separate out the data into mutually exclusive themes or groups prior to modelling.
22. Average price and distribution contributions illustrated in Figure 4.4 are incremental – expressed as short-term deviations from long-term trend. Long-term price and distribution trends are absorbed into the baseline during the decomposition process. It is these trends that are used in model (4.16).
23. Whereas the VAR technique is impractical in the context of the fully specified mix model due to the large number of variables generally involved, the focus on base sales evolution allows us to concentrate on a small group of variables, greatly simplifying the approach. Model (4.16) is derived from a VAR(1) specification – where all the variables appear with a one-period lag. The appropriate number of lags is generally tested such that each equation depicts a statistically congruent representation of the data.
24. Advertising data often comes in the form of TVR 'bursts' as illustrated in Figure 4.9. Under these circumstances, given the discrete nature of such data, it cannot be modelled as an endogenous variable in the system. Under these circumstances we would use (continuous) adstocked TVR data in (4.16) and condition on this (weakly exogenous) variable in estimation. Alternatively, we would transform the TVR data into a continuous Total Brand Communication Awareness variable.
25. To provide valid cointegrating relationships with base sales, other variables such as regular price, distribution and image statements must also be evolving. Advertising is generally stationary and would not enter the cointegrating relationship, reflected by the zero entries in the last column of the beta matrix above. The variable itself thus represents a stationary

'combination' and is represented by the third row in the beta matrix with $n-1$ restrictions, normalised on β_{73}.

26. Note that the regular price parameter estimate is distinct from the average price elasticity derived from the short-term mix model.

27. Note that shocks have to be identified as *structural* to ensure that they derive from the variable of interest and are not contaminated by effects from other variables in the system (see *inter alia* Juselius, 2006).

28. The underlying sales trend in equation 4.15(a) implies that marketing effects are orthogonal to the baseline. Thus, direct long-term marketing effects are zero by construction and any long-term effects are indirect – working through brand perceptions. An alternative approach, as discussed in Cain (2005) and exemplified in Osinga et al. (2009), is to specify the trend transition equation directly as a function of marketing effects thus allowing endogenous trend evolution.

29. Note that significant MA impact coefficients imply permanent or *hysteretic* indirect effects. Non-significant or zero coefficients do not, however, imply zero indirect effects. Even though the impulse response functions may decay to zero in the limit, any short- to medium-term impulse effects are still evidence of indirect marketing impacts – in addition to those measured in the short-term model.

30. Note that TV investments may serve to simply maintain base sales – with no observable impact picked up using time series econometric modelling. This can be dealt with by incorporating estimates of base decay in the absence of advertising investments – based on prior 'norms' or 'meta' analyses across similar brands in similar categories. Note also, that excessive price promotion may serve to increase price sensitivity by changing the consumer's price reference point. This constitutes an additional negative impact of price promotions on net revenues.

References

Almon, S. (1965), 'The distributed lag between capital appropriations and expenditures', *Econometrica*, 33 (January), 178–196.

Baghestani, H. (1991), 'Cointegration analysis of the advertising-sales relationship', *Journal of Industrial Economics*, 39 (6), 671–681.

Barten, A.P. (1966), *Theorie en empirie van een volledig stelsel van vraagvergelijkingen*, Doctoral dissertation, University of Rotterdam: Rotterdam.

Barten, A.P. (1969), 'Maximum likelihood estimation of a complete system of demand equations,' *European Economic Review*, 1, 7–73.

Binet, L. and Field, P. (2007), *Marketing in the Era of Accountability*, IPA Datamine, World Advertising Research Centre: London.

Broadbent, S. (1979), 'One Way TV Advertisements Work', *Journal of the Market Research Society*, 23, 3, 295–312.

Cain, P.M. (2005), 'Modelling and forecasting brand share: A dynamic demand system approach', *International Journal of Research in Marketing*, 22, 203–220.

Cain, P.M. (2008), 'Limitations of conventional market mix modelling', *Admap*, April, pp. 48–51.

Clarke, Darral G. (1976), 'Econometric measurement of the duration of advertising effect on sales', *Journal of Marketing Research*, 13, 345–357.

Deaton, A. and Muellbauer, J. (1980), *Economics and Consumer Behavior*, Cambridge University Press: Cambridge.

Dekimpe, M. and Hanssens, D. (1995), 'Empirical generalisations about market evolution and stationarity', *Marketing Science*, 14 (3), G109–G121.

Dekimpe, M. and Hanssens, D. (1999), 'Sustained spending and persistent response: A new look at long-term marketing profitability', *Journal of Marketing Research*, 36, 397–412.

Dickey, D.A. and Fuller, W.A. (1981), 'Likelihood ratio statistics for autoregressive time series with a unit root', *Econometrica*, 49, 1057–1072.

Givon, M. and Horsky, D. (1990), 'Untangling the effects of Purchase Reinforcement and Advertising Carryover', *Marketing Science*, 9 (2) (Spring), 171–187.

Granger, C.W.J. (1988), 'Some recent development in a concept of causality', *Journal of Econometrics*, 39, 199–211.

Harvey, A.C. (1989), *Forecasting, Structural Time Series Models and the Kalman Filter*, Cambridge University Press: Cambridge.

Houston, F.S., Kanetkar, V. and Weiss, D.L. (1992), 'Estimation procedures for MCI and MNL models: a comparison of reduced forms', unpublished working paper, University of Toronto: Ontario.

Jedidi, K., Mela, C. and Gupta, S. (1999), 'Managing advertising and promotion for long-run profitability', *Marketing Science* 18 (1), 1–22.

Johansen, S. (1996), *Likelihood-Based Inference in Cointegrated Vector Autoregressive Models, 2nd edn.* Advanced Texts in Econometrics, Oxford University Press: Oxford.

Juselius, K. (2006), The *Cointegrated VAR model: Methodology and Applications*. Advanced Texts in Econometrics, Oxford University Press: Oxford.

Koyck, L.M. (1954), *Distributed Lags and Investment Analysis*, North Holland: Amsterdam.

Mela, C., Gupta, S. and Lehmann, D. (1997), 'The long-term impact of promotion and advertising on consumer brand choice', *Journal of Marketing Research* 34 (2), 248–261.

Nakanishi, Masao and Cooper, Lee G. (1974), 'Parameter estimation for a multiplicative competitive interaction least squares approach', *Journal of Marketing Research*, 11, 303–311.

Osinga, Ernst C., Leeflang, Peter S.H. and Wieringa, Jaap E. (2009), 'Early marketing matters: A time varying parameter approach to persistence modelling', *Journal of Marketing Research*, XLV1, 173–185.

Schwert, G. William (1987), 'Effects of model specification on tests for unit roots in Macroeconomic data', *Journal of Monetary Economics*, 20 (1), 73–103.

Stone, J.R.N. (1954), 'Linear expenditure systems and demand analysis: An application to the pattern of British demand', *Economic Journal*, 64, 511–527.

Theil, H. (1965), 'The information approach to demand analysis', *Econometrica*, 33, 67–87.

5
The Secret of Successful Integrated Communication: Integrated Teams and ROI

Kelly Walsh

1 Introduction

Over the years MS&L has taken part in a number of integrated marketing communications (IMC) teams working on global, regional and local campaigns. This experience includes partnering with Leo Burnett and Philips to set up the first, fully integrated global marketing communication approach that went live in 2002. Since then MS&L have been involved in helping to set up over 20 integrated campaigns with clients spanning the consumer, corporate and healthcare sectors.

With the aim of sharing the wisdom gathered over the years I'd like to start with a definition of integrated IMC that explains how it should work:

> IMC is a process by which a client or brand leverages *all relevant* forms of communication to deliver a consistent expression of a product or brand values, positioning and message.

> At its heart lies a central *campaign idea* or thought which is co-created by a cross-discipline communications team. The campaign idea acts as the foundation of the brand communications programme and is relevant to all the brand's *stakeholders*.

However, the essential value of IMC can be expressed in the old adage 'The whole is greater than the sum of its parts'. The (seemingly) simple process of bringing senior experienced communications brains together under a holistic process produces an outcome far more powerful than any discipline could produce working as part of a loose federation.

In this chapter I will look at four pillars of success, outline a best practice model for IMC and share views on the benefits an IMC approach from both an agency and client perspective.

2   The Four pillars of success

Experience has taught us that there are four pillars that need to be in place in order for an IMC programme to deliver truly outstanding results.

2.1   Many disciplines, one leadership team

The more senior the IMC core team, the better. No matter which discipline you represent, you need to be empowered and confident to make important decisions quickly, with the experience behind you to guide that decision making. Inexperience, reticence or lack of confidence is quickly outed with the effect of marginalising that discipline (or person) and reducing the overall integrated impact.

It is important that each member of the IMC leads his or her discipline by example, keeping the bigger picture in mind at all times and demonstrating a willingness to make discipline concessions for the greater good of the campaign.

2.2   The right attitude

Next the team needs to come to the table with the right attitude – easy to say but very difficult to deliver. So what constitutes the right attitude?

> *Discipline proud but not prejudiced*: Team members might think their particular discipline is uniquely poised to answer the needs of the brief but that is very rarely the case. An inability to listen, consider and support other disciplines will derail the integration process and compromise the final result. Not all disciplines will make the final cut. Depending on the circumstances the traditional (above-the-line) ATL-led approach is not always going to be required and IMC core team members need to be able to identify and support the mix of marcom disciplines that are right for each situation.

Focused but not blinkered: An IMC team focused on a brief is usually working to a fairly tight deadline. Therefore it's imperative that they remain focused on the outcome but not to the extent that they are blinkered to those 'wild card' ideas that can elevate a campaign from good to great.

Critical but not judgemental: A good idea can come from anywhere and anyone – but not all good ideas will make it through the process. Each team member must come to the table determined to accept only the best thinking, but in a way that ensures the selection process is constructive and transparent. Whenever possible, key meetings should happen face-to-face as email and conference calls often produce situations where tone and intention can be misconstrued.

2.3 Co-creation

The right process can be summed up in one word – co-creation. Integration does not mean that all communications agencies are attached at the hip and operate as an inseparable unit throughout the whole of a campaign development and implementation process. However, there are key phases throughout the development process where all disciplines must come together as a co-creation team. While I'll go on to explain this in more detail in the following section, targeted co-creation delivers integration where it is needed most – bringing people together at the right time, in the right place, with the right outcome.

2.4 Client leadership and ownership

Without a client who fully supports a truly integrated process and is empowered to demand it from their agencies you are likely to descend straight into single discipline domination. As much as I'd like to say that all agencies enter this process holding hands and willing to share, that happens all too rarely. Depending on the channel focus of an IMC campaign, there will always be one agency that is set to lose out financially or will be asked to hand over the reigns of power for the duration of the campaign process. Without the client demanding that a channel neutral, co-creation process is followed the chances are the team will eventually defer to the traditional channel leader, thus compromising the outcome. Added to which the client could be missing out on unique opportunities and approaches that only a truly integrated approach can deliver.

3   A best practice IMC campaign development process

No two client companies operate an IMC campaign development process in the same way. This is further complicated by the fact that clients and participating agencies tend to develop weird and wonderful names for different stages of the same process. To simplify things I've focused on seven key stages that most IMC companies follow in order to produce a holistic campaign that will provide the best brand/variant experience for target consumers and business results for clients (see Figure 5.1).

The process should always commence with one marketing communications brief delivered by the client directly to the IMC team. Following the briefing the IMC team should meet to interrogate the brief and come back to the client with any questions or responses, as a single collective voice.

3.1   Loop springboard meeting

Cross discipline planners lead the IMC team in a process that identifies who the target audience is, how they behave, what interests

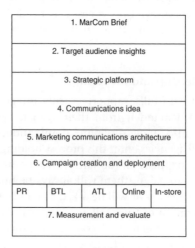

Figure 5.1   Producing a holistic integrated campaign

and influences them and when, where and how the target audience is most receptive to seeking out, receiving or disseminating information. In short, what consumer needs drive brand/variant choice.

This information provides the IMC team with a strong understanding of whom we are communicating with and identifies the most efficient and impactful route through to them. These insights are then made actionable via the strategic platform.

3.2   Strategic platform

The strategic platform is an articulation of the strategic consumer benefit. In other words it is the *performance and emotional equities that link the target consumer with the product*. Its purpose is to provide the direction for the creation of the central communications idea. It is not a creative strap line and chances are it will never appear in any form of copy that reaches the consumer. The process to arrive at the strategic platform tends to be led by the lead planner on the IMC team.

3.3   Communications idea

A common communication idea acts as the central architecture for the IMC campaign development and drives synergies across all consumer touch points. The creation process is led by the lead planner and involves input from all IMC team members to ensure its relevancy across disciplines.

3.4   Marketing communications architecture

This stage is the point at which the most relevant discipline channel selections are made based on the communications idea and target audience insights. Its purpose is to ensure that the target consumer is reached at the right time, in the right way, using the right medium. This process is usually led by the media agency with full IMC team consultation.

3.5   Campaign creation and deployment

Each relevant channel discipline will now independently develop their campaign programmes against the central strategic platform and communications idea. Throughout this process it is important that the IMC team comes together as a group to share thinking and ensure that the best ideas are captured and pulled through the line.

3.6   Measurement and evaluation

(This section is contributed by Clare Spencer from i to i tracker.)

3.6.1   *What's the point?*

When it comes to measuring and evaluating IMC, the fundamental principle is to know why you are doing it. In fact apply the same principle as you would at the outset of *planning* the IMC, be really clear on what success looks like.

I find it helpful to distinguish Measures of *Performance* (MOP) from Measures of *Effectiveness* (MOE). This is a distinction that the UK and the US military draw on when they are evaluating their communications, or PSYOPS as they label this, in theatres of war.

MOP speak to the success, or *efficiency* of the marketing agency in delivering the results; whether this relates to placing a media story or buying space, the measure is about the execution.

MOEs on the other hand speak to the success, or *effectiveness* of the activities on the target audience. There are many different models to measure such effectiveness but our particular approach has been developed with the key components of consumer success in mind.

3.6.2   *The i to i tracker® model*

The i to i tracker evaluation framework defines effectiveness at four levels (see Figure 5.2):

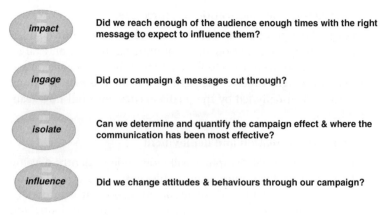

impact — Did we reach enough of the audience enough times with the right message to expect to influence them?

ingage — Did our campaign & messages cut through?

isolate — Can we determine and quantify the campaign effect & where the communication has been most effective?

influence — Did we change attitudes & behaviours through our campaign?

Figure 5.2   The 4 Is

The 'impact' module relies on secondary data, primarily reach and frequency data, and in the case of PR, analysis of message pick up by key media. The 'ingage', 'isolate' and 'influence' modules are based on primary research data.

3.6.3 Measurement in the round

The key benefit of this evaluation approach is that it measures 'in the round', assessing all communication – controlled or uncontrolled – related to the brand, service or issue. Clients often become hung up on knowing the ROI of their ad campaign, the impact of their shelf wobbler in-store or the Advertising Value Equivalent (AVE) of their PR campaign. This is a client-centric view of the world and does not reflect the real world of the consumer. The consumer is exposed to a multiplicity of messages, not all favourable nor placed by the client or Agency. Look at how Dell was decimated by the instant viral transmission via the Internet of an electrical fault on one of its laptops.

3.6.4 More than the sum of the parts

Another key component of this measurement approach is the ability to evaluate the integrated, or *additive effect* of the communication. By dint of using multi-channels, we achieved a greater effect than a single channel campaign.

At the end of the day, this should be what the client is striving to measure. Otherwise, they'd be better of using advertising as their sole activity.

The evidence is 'the more the merrier' when it comes to channels. From data-mining 880 case studies from the IPA/WARC database, and applying an effectiveness success rate (a proxy measure of 'large business effects', such as sales, market share, profit gain), the evidence is unequivocal. Multi-channel campaigns punch their weight (see Figure 5.3).

The average multi-channel campaign was significantly more effective in hard commercial terms than its single channel equivalent.

3.6.5 Measuring up?

However, what the multi-channel campaigns have in power, they lack in proof (see Figure 5.4). While we were able to extrapolate and quantify the business effects from the case studies, few of campaigns

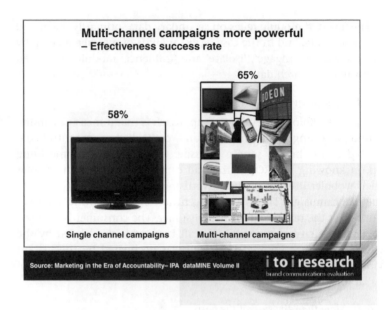

Figure 5.3　Multi-channel campaigns

had been evaluated 'in the round'. Although research was used in the majority of cases, it was primarily used to track intermediate measures, such as brand awareness and brand health and to track advertising effectiveness, and even then mainly TV. Only in a handful cases was any attempt made to evaluate the additive effect of the multi-channels.

3.6.6　Identifying the barriers

i to i research undertook interviews with ten Marketing Directors to establish some of the barriers to measuring in the round. The consensus was that while large-scale quantitative research enables robust evaluation of mass media, such as TV advertising, it precludes the pick-up of smaller-scale media, and activities.

For these, it is important to take a more micro-measurement approach, which can pick up smaller audience sizes, while offering the ability to still evaluate in the round. The approach i to i research takes is to dovetail the main survey vehicle with a grassroots methodology, such as a Web- or SMS-based survey. For example, if the client

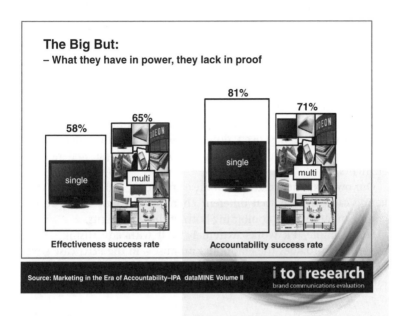

Figure 5.4   The big But

sponsors an event, such as Vinopolis, they will want to know not just how many people attended the event (an 'impact' measure) but how the event resonated and 'influenced' people. By contacting people via their mobile phones in real time when they are at the event you can gauge what their impressions are of the event, what messages they are picking up about the brand and products and what their likely behaviour is going to be. The trick is to then recruit them to partic- ipate in the main research survey to establish what other channels they were exposed to and whether their behaviour intent, for exam- ple to trial the brand, was realised. Typically, undertaken as an online survey, this second piece of research provides an all round picture of the effect of the IMC.

3.6.7   Emotional versus rational

One of the reasons that IMC are so successful is because they pull on the emotional and rational sides of our characters.

Emotionally based communication has been found to be the most successful, often because of the subliminal effects it has (reference Heath and Feldwick, Low Attention Processing thesis). The IPA DataMine report corroborated this by showing that campaigns that used emotional appeal – typically ad campaigns – were more likely to yield strong business results than rationally based ones which are founded more on information and persuasion principles.

However, little has been done to understand the effectiveness of multi-channel campaigns that combine emotional *and* rational elements.

Our own experience at i to i of measuring over 220 integrated marketing campaigns is that different channels can play different, but complementary roles combining both of these elements.

For example, PR works extremely well with advertising. While advertising provides the emotional promise – in the P&G case study below of 'gorgeous hair' – the PR underpins the promise by providing rational reasons to believe the advertising (see Figures 5.5 and 5.6).

Figure 5.5   PR enhances TV

Figure 5.6   PR teaser and reveal

The results of this campaign show that respondents were 65 per cent more likely to say they would purchase the brand if they recalled the Advertising (TV and Press) and the PR activities (see Figure 5.7).

3.6.8   Future evaluation?

More work is needed to better understand how channels work together to create more than the sum of their parts and which model of integration is optimal; for example, does a 'matching luggage' approach work best when the communications look, feel and say the same thing? Or is it better to have one campaign idea which is executed very differently?

3.6.9   Why integrated marketing communications works

There are a number of reasons why brands, companies and organisations should consider IMC as a way forward, but the overriding advantage is its ability to deliver a cross discipline winning strategic approach. By breaking down historical silos and getting the

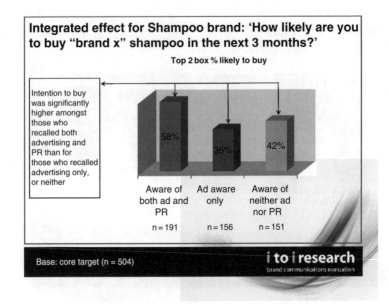

Figure 5.7   Integrated effect for shampoo brand

marcoms agencies together to address the challenges simultaneously, the resulting campaign is much more focused and single-minded.

A few of the advantages coming out of an IMC-focused approach:

- cross discipline buy-in from all stakeholders
- consistent through-the-line messaging
- more effective channel selection driven out of consumer insight and creative approach
- stronger creativity as the best ideas rise to the top and are applied across channels
- greater flexibility and willingness to leverage all communications opportunities
- greater value – one idea exploited holistically means less discipline/channel reinventing for the sake of it
- proven business builder demonstrating a higher campaign ROI

The IMC approach also delivers significant benefits to the PR/communications agencies involved. It is a much more inspirational and rewarding environment to work within as each member of the team has a seat at the table and the opportunity to lead the thinking. This intense level involvement gives the individuals in the team a greater sense ownership and pride in the results. The sharing of knowledge and approaches also enables every person around the table to learn and grow through exposure to best in class thinking. However, the biggest benefit lays in the fact that IMC campaigns deliver better, award-winning work that builds business that leads to bigger budgets and enables the IMC team to deliver more exciting solutions – a virtuous circle any marketing professional would want to be a part of.

6
Measuring Media Audiences and Using Media Research

Mark Balnaves

The accurate measurement of audiences is absolutely critical in modern integrated brand marketing. It is the starting point for assessing subsequent attitudinal or behavioural affects. Different media produce different types of audience statistics: TV, Internet, radio, POS. Different measures give you different insights into audience behaviour and the impact of particular media messages or campaigns on individuals or groups. Your return on investment in media and advertising and in any integrated communication approach will depend very much on an understanding of the potential and limitations of measurement. In this chapter we will look at contemporary issues impacting upon audience and media measurement, from current survey wars through to fractionation of audiences and media. The chapter will provide you with a basic introduction to different measurement designs for different media and the use of the statistics in different types of campaigns. The chapter will also give you insights into the future of measurement in media research and current thinking on directions.

1 Introduction

If the ruler doesn't work, we can't use it to measure the room and know how much carpet to buy...Radio was an effective medium and still is an effective medium – it is only the measurement that is not right.

(Ceril Shagrin, executive vice president,
corporate research, at Univision Communications)

When Hispanic advertisers and radio managers found that Arbitron's Personal People Meter (PPM) was significantly under reporting its Hispanic audience, compared with the Census (which also under reports Hispanic households), they were furious. Money rides on radio ratings – if you do not have any ratings for your radio station or programme then you do not have an audience to sell in the market. The matter went to court in 2009 and Arbitron reached agreements with the New York and New Jersey State Attorneys General to over-haul its ratings system to ensure that ethnic listeners are properly represented, including recruiting participants through a combina-tion of telephone number and address-based methods and increasing the number of cell phone-only households. The National Associa-tion of Black Owned Broadcasters (NABOB) and the Spanish Radio Association were required to fund a joint project to support ethnic radio.

The ways of knowing modern audiences – the methods of measure-ment – are now big billion dollar business, with Google in alliance with Nielsen, one of the world's leading media researchers, to liter-ally auction audiences off to the highest bidder. Ironically, 'the black box' of survey and sampling methodology that delivers audiences remains a mystery to most, just as Art Nielsen's original 'black box' – the Audimeter – for measuring radio sets baffled onlookers. How-ever, as the Hispanic and other minority broadcasters and marketers understood, marketing managers need to know both how audiences are measured as well as what the statistics from those measurements mean for their markets.

Understanding where the advertising $, £ or Euro goes, of course, is also important. Figure 6.1 shows variation in expenditure in each medium by different countries. In Ireland, as you can see, newspaper is still a major medium for advertising, whereas television dominates in Poland.

In media buying, the choice of a medium is dependent upon knowledge of who the audiences are and what they are watching, listening or reading. As we will see in this chapter, modern measure-ment of audiences is beset by a rapidly changing media and consumer environment, heightened demand for ever more precise informa-tion, increasing measurement difficulty and declining respondent participation. Sampling has also become the subject of political and methodological battles of how to represent people, including

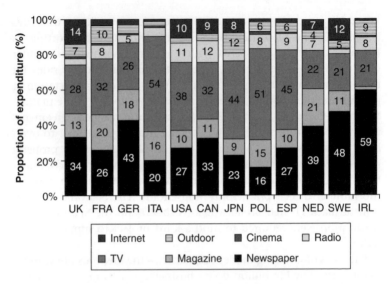

Figure 6.1   Advertising expenditure by medium and country

Source: Ofcom (2008).

everything from the Census to the Internet. Recent US research on non-response shows that technology-rich households are rejecting participation in audience surveys. The joint Arbitron and Nielsen Project Apollo designed to collect everything about audience and consumer behaviour also found the people were rejecting both the intrusion into their private lives and the tasks given to them. The aim of this chapter is to give you an insight into how measurements are used in media planning together with insights into their future. But whatever the future of the measurements might be, you will need to know about what measurements mean in any integrated brand marketing communication campaign.

2   Distorting measurement: Click fraud and hypoing

According to *The Independent* the advertising market in the United Kingdom experienced a significant shift in 2009 as companies for the first time spent more money on the Internet than on television. Spending on Internet advertising grew 4.6 per cent, or 23.5 per cent of the total market, in the first half of 2009 to £1.7 billion (Clark, 2009). Advertising on television by comparison was £1.6 billion, down from £1.9 billion in 2008. At the same time total advertising spend in the United Kingdom fell 3.5 per cent to £17.5 billion. Chief Executive of the Internet Advertising Bureau (IAB), Guy Phillipson, said that 'The results signal a significant restructure of marketing budgets as advertisers follow their audiences online and look to the internet for even more measurable and accountable methods' (Clark, 2009).

One might think that it is easy to measure what people do on the Internet, you simply track individual users – where they go and what they purchase. It is not that simple.

Life is good for 27-year-old Seth J. Sternberg. A year ago, he dropped out of Stanford Business School to work full-time on Meebo Inc., an easy-to-use service that has solved one of instant messaging's nagging problems: the inability to communicate with people who use an IM service other than yours. Today Meebo is going gangbusters. It has raised $3.5 million from the Silicon Valley crème-de-la-crème, including Marc Andreessen of Netscape fame and venture capital heavyweight Sequoia Capital. More impressively, the service attracts almost a million people every day, who swap more than 60 million messages. There's just one hitch: Sternberg and his co-founders have a hard time proving the site is as popular as they say it is. Look up Meebo's Web traffic using the comScore Networks Inc. service, and you'll find that a European competitor eBuddy.com is four times as big. Alexa, a competing Web measurement service owned by Amazon.com Inc. (AMZN), shows Meebo is bigger. Which is true? Probably neither. Sternberg's best guess is that the two rivals are about the same size. Yet even he doesn't know for sure.

(*BusinessWeek*, 2006)

Independent traffic analysts Nielsen NetRatings (NTRT) and comScore recruit Web surfers to record their mouse clicks. But when you log onto Meebo, instead of loading a new page for every mouse click, only the log-in section is loaded. No matter how long a person stays on Meebo they are viewing only one page. The metrics for the Internet are therefore by no means agreed. While expenditure on the

Internet may have increased there is no guarantee that an advertise-ment, for example, has the 'hits' claimed against it that various and often competing metrics might deliver. There is though an advan-tage in having an independent analysis of audience ratings. This has a long history.

In 1908 in Britain the Observer proceeded for damages against the Advertisers' Protection Society, formed in 1900 to ensure that man-ufacturers who paid for advertising would get better value for their money. Its first action was to invite newspaper owners to divulge cir-culation figures and when they refused they provided its members with private estimates for leading newspapers and journals. The Soci-ety had published an estimate of 5000 for the Observer's circulation. The Observer could show that its net sales were over 80,000, but the Society was acquitted, 'because, in the struggle for circulation which then consumed Fleet Street, there was no basis for more accurate estimates' (Harris and Seldon, 1954, p. 14). After this court case news-papers began publishing their circulation figures. The Society then embarked on a campaign for independently audited figures that led to the establishment of the Audit Bureau of Circulation in 1931. With the establishment of this Audit Bureau the principle of syndicated research had become established in a contested environment.

The temptation to distort measurement has remained. In broad-cast ratings distortion of results is called 'hypoing'. In the early days of radio ratings research some radio companies would try to dis-tort their ratings by holding competitions, or other events, at the time of ratings collection in order to increase their ratings. Archibald Crossley, the father of broadcast ratings, and his competitor C.E. Hooper, would ban radio stations from ratings collection if they were found to be involved in 'hypoing'. In an Internet environ-ment it is quite difficult to find out whether or not the 'ratings' have been distorted because there are so many factors that could cause distortion, ranging from companies astroturfing (pretending to be customers using a site), flogging (fake blogging), viral marketing through to problems with measurement or, indeed, private measure-ment companies systematically distorting the figures 'click [fraud]'. In broadcasting 'hypoing' came to a crisis with The Quiz Show scandal in the United States. The 1963 Congressional committee into broad-cast ratings established in the United States came about precisely because methodologists in the area of standards and measures in the

US Federal Government had concerns about how and what broadcast ratings companies were 'selling' to broadcast markets. Media company owners, including Lyndon Johnson, also had concerns about distortions in the market, especially in the wake of the Quiz Show scandal. The Quiz Show spiked ratings (hypoing) by rigging the success of one of its star performers by giving him the answers to all questions in advance. The subsequent Congressional Hearings, once they opened the 'black box' of broadcast ratings, started to discover some of its problems.

> The hearings suggested that the illusion of exact accuracy was necessary to the ratings industry in order to heighten the confidence of their clients in the validity of the data they sell. This myth was sustained by the practice of reporting audience ratings down to the decimal point, even when the sampling tolerances ranged over several percentage points. It was reinforced by keeping as a closely guarded secret the elaborate weighting procedures which were used to translate interviews into published projections of audience size. It was manifested in the monolithic self-assurance with which the statistical uncertainties of survey data were transformed into beautiful, solid, clean-looking bar charts'.
>
> (Bogart, 1966, p. 50)

The US Congressional committee also found that some of the audience ratings companies were completely bogus and not even conducting surveys (Bogart, 1966). The US committee was the first serious independent analysis of audience ratings methodology and conventions. It was also an important cultural marker because it signalled the first time that the auditing of broadcast ratings became systematic and from then on more or less taken for granted.

In Integrated Brand Marketing Communication (IBMC), therefore, it is important to understand the methods by which data are collected for each medium, the transparency of those methods, and the role of the research organisation that collects and analyses them. *Syndicated research* emerged precisely because of the need for a system that combined economical collection of data with minimum distortion. Nielsen ratings is used to calibrate other measurements because it relies on panels. The people chosen for those panels are known and selected as part of a major random sample. Understanding the nature of panels and samples is essential to an understanding of the whole measurement process.

3   Samples and panels

The survey panel was a revolution in the early twentieth century that transformed the collection of survey data. Panels are statistically representative groups of people or households that provide data to a study over time. In television ratings this longitudinal aspect has been fundamental to the operation of the business of ratings as it has provided the users of ratings with the capacity to map audience flow and to get a sense of what is happening to audiences over time. The process of selection of panels and their retention over time is there-fore key to the quality of data that is retrieved. In order to discuss the mechanics of selection of panels it is worthwhile briefly revisiting the very idea of random, probability, selections. Populations in statistical sampling are operationally defined by the researcher. They must be accessible and quantifiable and related to the purpose of the research. 'All households in Hull' is a definition of a population, with house-holds as the unit of analysis. But what is a 'household'? Is it any dwelling, including the boat in the backyard that your mother-in-law lives in? Is it the Hilton? If all of these examples are 'household', then these need to be included in the definition of the population. If a sample of households was drawn from Hull, then 'Hull' needs to be defined. Is Hull defined by local council boundaries? Is it defined by census boundaries? Traditionally, modern audience ratings com-panies have conducted establishment surveys and compared them against census data. The panel for television viewing, for example, is then drawn from those households defined as necessary for the panel. Not all households will be chosen but those households chosen, say about 4000–5000 households in countries like Australia, should be statistically representative of the population from which they were drawn.

When you have decided on all the definitions, then every house-hold that you have defined as a household belongs on your list. That list is called a *sampling frame*. You can number each household, if you wish, and put them in a hat (a big hat in this case). Let us say that you drew out 50 households (a sample). You know that there was no bias in your choice. Each element, each household, in your sampling frame had an equal chance of being chosen. This is called *a probability or random sample.* You could of course swap your hat for a computer and use a table of computer-generated random numbers for selection.

Large-scale, national studies often use a form of cluster sampling called multi-stage cluster sampling. Normally we select one unit at a time in probability sampling. This requires a complete list of the units of analysis. Sometimes there is no way to create a list. In these cases we use a procedure known as cluster sampling. In cluster sampling we select groups or categories. For example, following Figure 6.2, we can break Hull up into suburbs and randomly sample those suburbs.

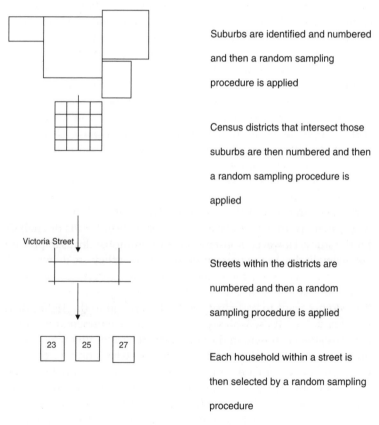

Suburbs are identified and numbered and then a random sampling procedure is applied

Census districts that intersect those suburbs are then numbered and then a random sampling procedure is applied

Streets within the districts are numbered and then a random sampling procedure is applied

Each household within a street is then selected by a random sampling procedure

Figure 6.2   Multi-stage cluster sampling – Following the census tracts

Table 6.1   Random selection from households for interview

Person to interview	No. of People in Household				
	1	2	3	4	5
	1	2	2	4	3
		1	1	2	5
			3	1	4
				3	1
					2

We could then break up those suburbs into census collectors' districts (about 400 households) and then randomly select those districts. We could then select households using systematic random sampling in those streets. A systematic sample is when every _n_th unit of analysis is selected – every second house in the street, for instance. Once we have selected the households we would then select the demographic quota from those households. In order to randomly select our participants from households we could again use a table of random numbers, Table 6.1. For example, the interviewer could ask, 'How many people are there in your home aged 15 or older?' If the first participant says '3 people', then according to Table 6.1 the second oldest person is chosen (Balnaves, 2001).

If it is not possible to get an appropriate sampling frame, or list, then a researcher can use other non-statistical means of selection or vary the definition of the population. This is often done in the case where there is unlikely to be a full accessible list of units of analysis for the study. However, non-random, or non-probability, samples are *not* generalisable to the population from which they are drawn.

Television ratings panels may obtain an appropriate sampling frame but that is not the end of it. If not all the 'basics' – those on the list – do not want to participate, as Nielsen found in the 1990s, then the alternatives, those who say yes, may not be representative of the panel originally chosen. In the case of Nielsen's the 'alternates' ended up having less televisions and were heavier television viewers than the 'basics'. There end up being key tradeoffs if an appropriate statistically representative group cannot be found. Table 6.2 provides a summary of those tradeoffs. The ultimate in survey research is to gain a Data Rich and Case Rich outcome. Data Rich means that the information coming back from the audience is extensive and has qualitative

Table 6.2 Trade offs in the underlying survey ways

	Case Rich	Case Poor
Data Rich	Single source (the Holy Grail)	Custom
Data Poor	Syndicated	Quick and dirty

Source: Miller (2009).

depth. For example, information on Facebook is Data Rich – there is significant information posted by people on to their sites that can be used to understand audiences and what they think or do. However, it is very difficult to establish from Facebook an appropriate sampling frame or probability sample that allows researchers to generalise their findings. Facebook has millions of users. These 'users' do not form into well-defined and easily accessible lists. There are as a result problems in establishing or verifying identities of users and creating an acceptable list where a random draw or stratification can be made. Facebook, therefore, is Data Rich but Case Poor as an audience and as a source of information. The traditional panel for television ratings, by contrast, is Case Rich and Data Poor. The Data Poor nature of the television ratings measured by exposure – who watches, where, for how long – was made up by the fact that users of the ratings found them practical and acceptable as a form of currency (a trade off). Miller (2009) would call this part of the 'coordination rule' in audience ratings. There was in the past confidence that the television ratings panel indeed reflected the population from which it was chosen. Through Peoplemeters the television ratings panels have provided information about an audience's *exposure* to television. If a company or a researcher wants more information about whether the audience actually like programmes, then customised Data Rich studies are often required. Modern syndicated ratings research therefore has often complemented by customised studies seeking more detailed information about audiences.

In summary, Case Rich studies are those that use statistical sampling methods to derive their samples from sampling frames. Case Poor studies are those that have not deployed statistical sampling methods and therefore their samples cannot be used to represent the populations from which they might have been drawn. Data Rich studies are those that yield detailed data or accounts from participants. In the case of television, for example, an interviewer living with a television household for a month is getting fine-grained qualitative data. Data Poor studies are those that gain minimal information back for their purpose. In the case of television ratings, exposure gives the media industry basic information about who is watching, when and for how long. Those studies that do not gain an appropriate probability, statistical sample and do not gain particularly rich and detailed information are both Data Poor and Case Poor. The modern problem for syndicated research is that participants do not want to participate, especially those who are of most interest to media researchers. If panels are failing to adequately represent the modern audience, then they are Case Poor. The data as a result are not generalisable to the defined population.

Broadcast ratings did not and does not deliver *single source* data. It is not the Holy Grail. It is, as discussed, a compromise. The sampling is Case Rich but the measure, exposure, provides the minimum acceptable data back for decision-making in the media industry. In fact, advocates of single source, such as John Philip Jones (1995), found a startling conclusion from research on exposure.

> one exposure generates the highest proportion of sales, and additional exposures add very little to the effect to the first. The advertising-response function is concave-downward, demonstrating diminishing returns in the clearest possible way. Effective frequency is provided by a single exposure. It is wasteful to concentrate media money into 'flights' to provide an average of more than one "Opportunity-to-See" (OTS).
>
> (1195:11)

The attempt to get to single source data will, doubtless, continue (Jones, 1995).

Helen Crossley was Archibald Crossley's daughter. She worked with her father in radio ratings and then later in public opinion polling. She recounts her early experience as a child in calculating radio ratings:

> My father would bring them home, interview cards, and he trained me how to do tabulate data from them – 1, 2, 3, 4 across, 1, 2, 3, 4 across, to make bunches of fives that could be added up by hand.

I got into that by the time I was 10. I remember that there were four radio networks across the top of the sheet, and you put your check mark under whichever network the listener was reporting, so when you added them all up and counted them in piles of five, you knew how many listeners you had out of 20 calls.

(Helen Crossley, 2008)

Helen Crossley is without a doubt the first child to tabulate the first audience ratings. She is an icon of the American Association for Public Opinion Research (APPOR). Archibald Crossley was the founder of Crossley ratings and for all intents and purposes the founder of audience ratings (Beville, 1985). Helen Crossley helped her father in audience ratings research and later in public opinion polling research. Archibald Crossley measured *exposure* in his radio ratings analysis. Exposure has become the *standard way* – the convention – for measuring broadcasting ratings. In Australia Bill McNair and his competitor George Anderson set up competing ratings systems in the 1940s and developed, like their counterpart Crossley in the United States, measures of *exposure*. McNair like Crossley used interviews, initially recall of programmes listened to and later coincidental, calling at the time of listening. Anderson used diaries. Syndicated research – ratings numbers based on estimates of exposure delivered to subscribers – remains the key factor in making decisions on buying and selling media space. Exposure measures, simply, whether an audience has been exposed to a programme and for how long. It does not measure whether the audience likes a programme or what kinds of engagement or attention might be involved in exposure (even though these are most likely inferred from length and repetition of viewing, of course).

The advantage of the ratings has been in the delivery of a 'single number' for use in media buying and selling. The advantage of panels and probability samples has been in their ability to represent with a fair degree of accuracy the demographics from which they are drawn. As media and media use have become more fragmented, so has the need to establish panels to represent each medium. Table 6.3 provides a summary of panels that Nielsen runs as part of its A2M2, anytime anywhere strategy.

Project Apollo is the paradigm example of an attempt to capture everything people do in one panel. When Nielsen and Arbitron

Table 6.3 Nielsen Panels

	Year	Households in panel	Location
National Peoplemeter	1987	14,000	US
Local Peoplemeter	2002	600–800	US in 13 markets
Set Metered Markets (Electronic boxes that track viewing but information about the view is in a diary)	1959	21,000	US
Hispanic People Meter Supplement	1994	270	US
Out of Home (Measures TV viewing at work, bars, airports, and so on, using sounds from the programmes that are recorded automatically by special mobile phones)	2008	4,700	US
Homescan Global (Purchasing behaviour)	1988	135,000	27 countries
Homescan US consumers	1988	125,000	US
Homescan Hispanic	2007	2,500	US/Latin America
FANLinks (Cross-references Homescan with their fan interests)	2005	50,000	US
Project Apollo (Multimedia consumption and purchasing – now cancelled)	2006	5,000	US
Nielsen BookScan (US book industry data)	2001	12,000 Booksellers	US
Your Voice (Online community for opinions)	2000	500,000+	Global
Nielsen Mobile Bill Panel (Activity on mobiles)	2005	20,000 Mobile bills	US
Hey! Nielsen (Website where users rate TV shows, movies, and so on)	2007	30,000	US
NetView & MegaPanel (Offline and online audience and market research)	1997	475,000	US and 9 other countries

Table 6.3   (Continued)

	Year	Households in panel	Location
Pine Cone Research (Product and concept surveys)	1999	173,000	Global
The Hub (Former members of other panels who allow Nielsen to track them)	2008	1,000	US

Source: Story (2008).

joined forces to set up the experimental Project Apollo in 2005 they expected to capture all of the everyday behaviour of audiences, from reading papers through to using mobile phones and buying food. To their surprise they found that people did not want to participate. The more they were asked to do and to provide, the more they resisted and refused. The current situation involves many separate panels for separate activities, for example a panel for outdoor advertising, a panel for mobile phones, and so on.

Researchers do have access to 'buyer graphics' such as actual purchases of, say, food and books. Nielsen's Scantrack, Infoscan (IRI) and Scan America (Control Data) that market High Tech Single Source use meters to measure television viewing and track supermarket product purchase. The failure of Project Apollo and the recent Nielsen study, however, points to the problems of tradeoffs in the quality of data that is happening. Getting people to scan each of their products purchases and to participate in other data collection activities is not easy.

One methodological option is *fusion* – to fuse data across the different panels, comparing all those demographics drawn from different sampling frames and then treating them as the same. But, as you might guess, this has inbuilt risks associated with it, especially at a time where media use can vary significantly within what look like similar demographic segments.

Audience ratings panels and survey research generally have always had problems with non-response or non-participation in research, even in the days of Archibald Crossley, Hans Zeisel and Paul Lazarsfeld. However, the continued erosion of the ability to get people to participate or to give more data about themselves represents genuine difficulties in attaining quality data at the very time when there is today an explosion in demands for more measurement.

4   The problem of non-response bias

Nielsen conducted a non-response bias study in 2009, the first of its kind, and its results give an insight into the role of the modern audience in survey research and the limits the audience itself puts on participation. The study consisted of 2300 basics, with 1000 responding households (a 95 per cent return rate) and 1300 refusing households (a 62 per cent return rate). Special in person follow ups were made with those households that did not respond. Few studies have followed up with non-responding households on why they have not participated or given data and this is what makes this particular study important. Miller (2009) found that there were significant differences between responding and refusing households for the 8–11 p.m. daypart, with the possibility of differences in the 5–9 a.m. daypart. Comparisons of differences by channels showed significant differences for CNN, HBO with MTV and Fox approaching significance. But it is the figures in Table 6.4 that surprised researchers and start to show why many people do not want to participate in modern audience panels and audience ratings survey panels especially. Nielsen found that technology-rich households did not want to participate in research – the very demographic that modern marketers want to grab. In this case, those with big screens,

Table 6.4   Equipment comparisons

Device	% Refuse	% Response	P value
Big Screen	22.6	41.2	0.00
Cable	61.9	69.1	0.00
Satellite	24.7	28.5	0.18
DVR	9.7	20.1	0.00
Hi Speed Web	72.9	75.3	0.30
Web TV	63.6	69.5	0.15
3+ TVs	46.1	60.2	0.00

Source: Miller (2009).

cable, DVR and three or more televisions did not want to participate. There are various reasons for this non-participation, ranging from an unwillingness of households to allow increased intrusion into their lives across a range of technologies and, of course, the simple fact that the technologies themselves need to be intruded upon in order to gain data (e.g., additional wiring) and participants do not want their expensive technology tampered with in any way. Traditionally, audience research companies appealed to the civic duty of participants in coming on to a panel and, indeed, participants held that coming on to a panel was a contribution to democracy. This has given way today to appeals as a consumer and reward.

The results of the Miller study highlight the need for Integrating Marketing Communication (IMC) scholars and practitioners to keep an eye on the fate of the panel and any major random sampling exercise and to seek data from research providers on non-response.

5   Alternatives to the panel (and replacing people with technology)

The early ratings methodologies used families and social class definitions to segment the audience. McNair and Anderson even ran different definitions of the audience up until 1963. McNair used A, B, C, D, E and Anderson used A, B, C (upper, middle, industrial). The age categories for television were also different. The aim of this methodology was to produce relatively simple data for the production of figures for buying and selling data. The use of social class definitions affected the 'argot' or local language for reporting audience ratings. The term 'AB', for example, began in 1959 in one of McNair's January/February reports when he started using Class AB (without separating them, as the company had done in previous reports).

The Peoplemeter was a new method for the measurement and collection of data and emerged in the 1980s as a way of capturing from households viewing information nearly all the time and transferring it directly from a set top box on the television to a computer. Interestingly diaries are still used for the Australian radio market but Peoplemeters for the most part dominate television. The Peoplemeter did not radically alter the classifications of the audience but it did introduce greater expectations of speed of delivery of the results of audience ratings. Electronic audience ratings allowed collection of the data nearly all the time and for users of ratings to manipulate the results using software packages created for this purpose.

What has changed since McNair and Anderson's time is proliferation of media and fragmentation of audiences. In the United States, United Kingdom and Australia this has led to a new challenge to the audience ratings convention. Of particular interest in Australia is Foxtel and regional Pay-TV group Austar, in conjunction with MCn, announcing in 2008 the launch of a new digital television audience measurement system (AMS) that would, the group argued, be the largest measurement system in Australia, providing viewing results from a panel of 10,000 Australian subscription TV homes (Bodey, 2008). The system is designed to give the Pay-TV group information on how Australians are adapting to the digital TV environment, the acceptance of the new standard definition and high definition multi-channels and trends in time-shifted viewing (Bodey, 2008).

The interesting thing is that there is now measurement of many media, from use of mobiles through to television, but there is no agreement on a currency that covers all the measurements. In the original broadcast ratings convention audiences were relatively stable and there were few media. An audience 'rating' reflected an audience that had critical mass and was, hopefully, for example, watching or listening to the medium. What has occurred is that the media industry has decided to do more measurement without a corresponding standard emerging. This is, if you like, more statistics but without a convention.

The broadcast audience ratings convention, or compact, has had several important components (Balnaves and O'Regan, 2009). The convention at base:

1. has exposure as the key measurement;
2. must appeal to the inherent correctness of the measurement;
3. uses a probability, statistical, sample;
4. delivers a 'single number';
5. is syndicated to reduce costs to subscribers;
6. has generally been Third Party;
7. is expected to work in the public interest (i.e., accurately represent the public audience).

Media ratings systems have traditionally provided an economic foundation for advertiser-supported media. Consequently the nature of the audience measurement process affects the structure and behaviour of media companies and regulators alike. Changes in the techniques and technologies of the ratings have 'a significant effect on the economics of media industries (because these changes can affect advertiser behaviour), the relative economic health of various segments of the media industry, and the nature of the content that media organisations provide' (Napoli, 2003, 65).

Although changes to the ratings convention governing audience measurement can be disruptive, these changes are driven by the inevitable gap between the measured audience and the actual audience for a service or programmes. With the advent of a more diverse and fragmented media environment and fractionated audiences, increasingly demographically defined, this gap has become even more evident with the validity of ratings as currency for buying and selling media being challenged in the United States. Napoli (2003) suggests that this is leading to a decline in quality and value of the 'audience product' – data on who is watching when – because of changes in technology and audiences.

Determining the popularity of programmes remains an important reason for ratings research whether for traditional broadcasting or the Internet. Given the problems with modern panels and the use of exposure as a measure, attention has turned to the 'quality' of the audience in addition to their size, as content providers and advertisers seek both to know their audiences/consumers better and to hone in on those considered most 'valuable'. The scheduling aspect of ratings remains important in 'traditional' television (FTA and STV), although time-shifting whether via 'catch-up channels' on STV, or through use of DVRs, and the increasing availability of content online has to some extent eroded the importance of the schedule. Having said this, it is clear that scheduling decisions are still made by networks, broadcasters and narrowcasters in part at least through consideration of the ratings of a particular programme, or in the case of new programmes the performance of other similar programmes. 'Hammocking' – the practice of scheduling a programme before, after or between high-rating programmes in order to maintain an audience – is an instance of scheduling decisions determined by ratings. This practice is however becoming more and more difficult as the audience's availability may be dispersed across time, or determined by factors other than the push-driven schedule. Creating a market for advertising has historically been one of the principal purposes of ratings, or of high rating shows.

All the evidence points to how difficult this is becoming for television providers and media buyers as the market is more fragmented than ever. Broadcast television's share of the advertising revenue pie is decreasing as other platforms and services attract viewers and hence become more attractive for advertisers. Neuromarketing, proprietorial registration systems, small audiences, zero ratings, fusion – all these terms or phrases signify a different type of audience ratings convention or measurement and a search for alternatives to exposure as the main metric and the panel as the mainstay for data collection. Neuromarketing today includes everything from measuring eye-gaze to galvanic skin response. In early advertising research it would have been called 'motivational research'. Customised studies often complement syndicated research in order to understand attitudinal or behavioural characteristics that might not be captured in the measured used for syndicated delivery. With television programmes, for example, a customised study might look at self-report responses on whether or not people liked a programme or, as in the case of Disney's Media Lab in Houston, explore eye-gaze, heart beat and galvanic skin response to complement self-report.

Replacing self-report from people with technology as the main reporting instrument is another option. For example, Aribtron, the monopoly provider for radio ratings in the United States, has for many years been trying to replace the paper diary with a PPM (Personal People Meter). The PPM is like a pager. It can pick up digital codes from different media and send the information to a database. Arbiton has used paper and pencil diary systems for radio since 1965. But the Australia radio broadcasting market rejects the technology push. Australia's Commercial Radio Australia argues that the PPM:

- Costs 2 to 3 times the cost of the diary system
- Has no real evidence of long-term compliance across all demographics,for example, once listening is lost, it is lost and cannot be regained
- Drops in breakfast listening have been recorded in trials with no valid evidence provided for device purveyors' explanation that

'people must have been over-reporting breakfast listening'! 'And industry does not accept this explanation as no other daypart has been supposedly over-reported. We do not believe that tens of millions of diary keepers across the world over the last 50 years have all over-reported breakfast and no other daypart' (Commercial Radio Australia 2008).

At the time of writing this paper, Nielsen Australia were – ironically – invited by radio broadcast networks in the United States to bring its diary into the US radio market, in competition with Arbitron. But regardless of the technology versus self-report (diary) argument (Gluck and Pellegrini, 2008), if a properly constituted panel cannot be obtained then the industry is stuck with Case Poor Data Poor (quick and dirty). Neuromarketing and engagement are possible alternative metrics, but if there is no statistically representative sample then the industry will be relying on Data Rich Case Poor. At present, though, there is no agreed upon metrics for neuromarketing and if history is a guide then it is unlikely that there can be.

The other major trend in the contemporary moment is to buy large audiences. Google bought YouTube in 2006 for $1.65 billion. At that time YouTube had over 100 million videos viewed every day and over 72 million individual visitors each month. Google has made its money from small text advertisements displayed next to Google search results. These advertisements deliver most of Google's US$16.6 billion in revenue. This is a different model from traditional audience measurement and delivery of advertising to audiences. Google's approach is to buy massive audiences and to experiment with them. It does not need panels or samples because it has either a record of what its users do or a site like YouTube, where the audience gathers. That audience in itself has economic value. This is a proprietary model and with it comes the dream of measuring the 'total' audience – no random sampling. Google's main advertising revenue, however, remains the spot advertisements on its Web pages.

6   Reach and frequency

On the media side of the equation, media analysis tools have been developed for the assessment of the reach and frequency associated with different media and the costs to be charged against them. Reach refers to unduplicated exposures or gross impressions and the number of different people exposed to the message. Frequency refers to the average number of exposures and how many times an audience is exposed to a message. Outdoor, newspapers, magazines tend to be the best media for frequency. Broadcast advertising and magazines tend to be the best for reach. The best combination is found in radio.

A cost per thousand (CPM) calculation is made how much it costs to deliver 1000 gross impressions or to reach 1000 listeners, viewers, readers, households and so on. CPM allows media planners to compare media based on audience and cost. The lowest CPM medium therefore is the most efficient.

For print media when the cost of the advertisement is known:

$$CPM = \frac{\text{Cost of advertisement} \times 1000}{\text{Circulation}}$$

when audience data are available:

$$CPM = \frac{\text{Cost of 1 advertisement} \times 1000}{\text{Number of readers reached}}$$

For broadcast media based on homes reached by a given programme or time period:

$$CPM = \frac{\text{Cost of 1 commercial} \times 1000}{\text{Number of homes reached}}$$

There is no editorial environment for outside media use, unlike television, radio, newspaper and the Internet. In television research a person might remember what they have seen by reference to the name of a programme. Outdoors, however, a person might not be able to give the same kind of response to what they have seen. Nielsen has a panel looking at out of home media use, but there are also dedicated measurements for signage.

Outdoor measurement normally counts the number of vehicles and people driving or walking down roads. An audit of the characteristics of advertising panels is made for which the researchers require an audience measure. Researchers then identify travel patterns and correlate these to the known locations of poster sites. A calculation is made of how many people go past a poster panel and how often they do so. This is called the opportunity to see (a gross OTS). Programmes like Postar in Britain also undertake a Visibility Study eye-tracking study to adjust the OTS to get a net figure.

Broadcast media measure exposure – attention – and provide the ability to analyse audience flow, or cumulative reach; how audiences or customers are built over time. Print media do not have the same capability in their metrics. Readership research, as customised research within print media, can provide insights into readership behaviour and which content may be popular or unpopular. Unlike broadcast media, print media metrics make assumptions about additional numbers of individuals who read a publication in addition to its purchase. This is reasonable because more than one person in a household, for example, is likely to read a newspaper even if it has been purchased just once. The metrics, however, do not deliver amount of time spent over a period of time, something broadcast media do provide.

A typical media evaluation will give you a breakdown of the circulation and audience or readership with a message average for each medium. Various software packages are also available for organisations to work out optimum planning for delivery of messages and campaigns. These programmes draw from syndicated data, like television ratings, and other sources. Figure 6.3 provides a brief example of AdQuest software that analyses Australia's ATR/OzTam

Figure 6.3 Software analytics in media planning

television ratings data and Roy Morgan and OMD packages that provide additional analytical tools, including psychographics.

Of course, all these data analysis tools will deliver a figure regardless of the analyser's ability to know when standard deviations are making the figures meaningless. The early advertising agencies often had senior practitioners who were expert methodologists – the psychologist J.B. Watson with JWT; Hans Zeisel, Paul Lazarsfeld and many others. They knew the limitations of the data that they were dealing with. Indeed, the agencies themselves did the research. One of the major historical changes to agencies was the outsourcing of audience and marketing research. This outsourcing had two effects over time: (i) expertise in methodology in house declined – modern media buyers, for example, are normally lowly paid number crunchers (Webster et al., 2000); and (ii) the close relationship between advertising agencies and their clients in accessing and using client sources of data changed. The modern media environment, ironically, is forcing agencies to revisit their historical roots. As syndicated research enters new, untested territory, in-house data that companies might derive from their own customers becomes more important. Pay-TV services, for example, are measuring their own subscribers and using syndicated research to calibrate those data. The relationship between syndicated research agencies and Pay-TV companies has become slightly problematic. The temptation to begin 'hypoing' will become almost irresistible among Pay-TV providers in a climate where proprietary measures abound with no convention to bond them. Pay-TV revenue in Europe and the United States now exceeds traditional advertising revenue. The apparent decline in the media advertising dollar has already been widely reported.

Budgets were revised down for the seventh consecutive quarter, with only 10% of companies surveyed revising their 2009 marketing budgets upwards. 38% reported a reduction. Despite the slowing rate of decline, the majority of categories suffered downward revisions in Q2 2009 – main media advertising dropped 18.4%, internet advertising was down 7.9%, sales promotion fell 8.8% and direct marketing was revised downwards by 7.5%. The only media category whose rate of decline accelerated was internet search; yet it remains the most resilient category with a 5.4% fall.

(Bold, 2009)

If we look briefly at the fragmentation of the media market in the United States alone, then we can get a sense of why decisions on directing the advertising dollar are complex. There is a much longer tail with modern media than there was in the past. In the 1920s and 1930s Archibald Crossley could be fairly confident that the whole family was listening to one radio in the living room – in Australia families would lie down on the floor, switch off the lights, and listen to the drama. Companies like Unilever, selling soap and detergent, dominated the market. The audience today can be anywhere from Twitter to playing World of Warcraft.

1985
3 Networks
7744 Radio Stations
2722 Print Options
4 Outdoor Forms

2008
7 Networks VOD
12,718 Radio Stations DVD
12,709 Print Options (H)DTV
150+ Cable Networks Database
500 Digital Channels Digital Cable
Interactive TV IPTV
Gaming Internet
Podcasting Email
Video Ads Mobile
Virtual Communications Advergaming
Social Networking Widgets
Twitter (microblogging) Social/Mobile
Search

Media and advertising industry analysts started to uniformly put forward figures in 2007 arguing that below the line advertising has expanded at the cost of media advertising. Table 6.5 gives an overview of non-traditional compared with traditional media. Some estimates by analysts put the advertising revenue pie split at 65 per cent non-traditional (Kirby, 2007). Booz Allen Hamilton provided a US comparison of traditional versus non traditional media expenditure, presented in Figure 6.4.

168

Table 6.5 Shifting away from traditional advertisements

Non-Traditional	Traditional
Media	Local Newspapers
Event Marketing	Local Radio
Premiums/Promotions	Local TV
P-O-P Displays	Local Yellow Pages
Internet (Email, SEM)	Other Local Media
Sponsorships	National TV Networks
Coupons	Cable TV
Specialty Printing	Magazine
Licensing	Spot TV
Agency Net Revenues	Newspapers
Public Relations	National Radio
Loyalty	Syndication TV
Games, Contests,	Yellow Pages
Sweeps	Other National Media
Product Sampling	Telephone Marketing
	Direct Mail

Source: Kirby, S.F. How Traditional Media Can Survive, Monetize and Grow Profits in the Digital Age. Interep NAB.

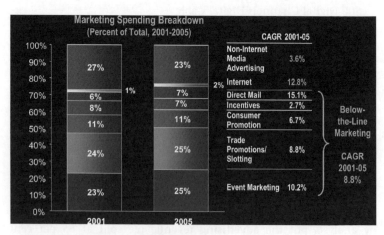

Figure 6.4 Traditional versus non traditional media advertising comparison (US)

Source: Vollmer and Rothenberg (2007).

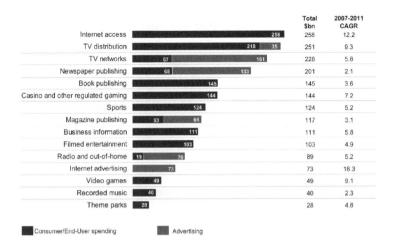

	Total $bn	2007-2011 CAGR
Internet access	258	12.2
TV distribution	251	9.3
TV networks	228	5.8
Newspaper publishing	201	2.1
Book publishing	145	3.6
Casino and other regulated gaming	144	7.2
Sports	124	5.2
Magazine publishing	117	3.1
Business information	111	5.8
Filmed entertainment	103	4.9
Radio and out-of-home	89	5.2
Internet advertising	73	18.3
Video games	49	9.1
Recorded music	40	2.3
Theme parks	28	4.6

■ Consumer/End-User spending   ■ Advertising

Figure 6.5 Consumer end-user spending and advertising, estimates 2007–2011

Source: Entertainment and Media Outlook. 2007–2011. PricewaterhouseCoopers, October.

The shift to below the line advertising is, no doubt, encouraged by the notion that the metrics for those formats are much closer to engagement, compared with exposure, and a perceived better measure for ROI. PriceWaterhouse Coopers estimates for consumer spending compared with advertising spend, Figure 6.5, show an interesting picture against each medium.

Certainly, traditional and non-traditional media vehicles are combined in modern campaigns. Caemmerer's (2009) report on how Renault and Nordpol + Hamburg executed its integrated communication campaign is a contemporary example of how media and evaluation are used in tandem. The objective of the campaign was to increase consumer awareness of the safety of Renault cars with the message: 'Die sichersten Autos kommen aus Frankreich' ('The safest cars come from France'). The campaign used cinemas, the Internet, television and print. Figure 6.6 shows the media campaign schedule:

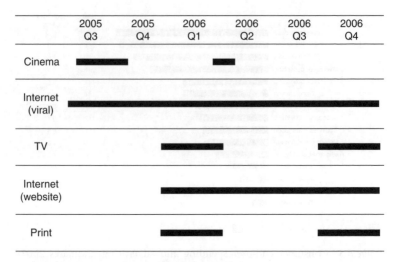

	2005 Q3	2005 Q4	2006 Q1	2006 Q2	2006 Q3	2006 Q4
Cinema	▬▬▬			▬		
Internet (viral)	▬▬▬▬▬▬▬▬▬▬▬▬▬▬▬▬▬▬▬▬▬▬▬▬▬▬▬					
TV			▬▬▬			▬▬▬
Internet (website)			▬▬▬▬▬▬▬▬▬▬▬▬▬▬▬			
Print			▬▬▬			▬▬▬

Figure 6.6   Renault media campaign schedule
Source: Caemmerer (2009).

TNS Sofres was employed to track changes in consumer attitudes and to evaluate the effectiveness of the campaign. The study showed an increase in awareness levels of the safety of Renault cars, from 44 to 52.2 per cent and intentions to purchase a car from Renault. According to Caemmerer (2009) an independent readership survey by the magazine *Auto-Motor-und-Sport* also showed that Renault had achieved a 7 per cent increase in consumer perception of safety. The Renault campaign is a good example of tactical use of media all focussed on a single coherent message. The Director of Marketing at Renault held that Cinema was a good venue for high-quality film and advertisements. The combination of the media is assumed to enhance reach and frequency to the desired target demographics, but Renault had no metrics to see which medium might have been more influential than another or indeed, how the viral marketing might have been taken up either within other Internet forums or in other media.

What this raises, which is not new in areas like Customer Relationship Management (CRM) of course, is how organisations like Renault might establish an ongoing monitoring and relationship with its customers 'inside' rather than the employment of one off campaigns and then evaluation 'outside'. It also then raises the question of relationship of IMC agencies to their clients in terms of the data that clients might have on their customers. This is precisely why Pay-TV companies want to know their own customers well, and over time, and use syndicated sources like Nielsen as calibration tools (Miller, 1994). Evaluation and the technology of research are built into the business model and, importantly, are longitudinal.

7 Media measurement and consumer behaviour

The benefit of panels in broadcast television ratings has been in the ability to economically understand audience flow and cumulative reach – how audiences or customers build over time. This enables strategists to decide not only the audiences or customers they want but also those audiences they do not want. It is worthwhile putting into summary some of the issues that we have discussed.

1. Surveys and panels are under pressure for a range of reasons, non-response being one of them. There is a sampling frame revolution under way where it is not clear how lists are going to be acquired, or panels maintained, threatening Case Rich data;
2. There is a fractionation of audiences, media and consumer products;
3. There appears to be a decline in media advertising and an expansion of below the line advertising. There is instability in the convention that exposure – attention – is the basic measure in broadcast media research. Motivational research and engagement are perceived as an alternative metric to exposure;
4. The metrics for new media like the Internet are not settled – there is no convention for them in the same way that there is a convention for exposure;
5. There is unlikely to emerge a 'single number' to cover all media, because of practical difficulties in getting people to participate in any research that does so;
6. In broadcast media, Pay-TV revenue now exceeds traditional advertising revenue in Europe and the United States. Many companies in the media industry – such as Pay-TV – are developing

their own metrics, independently of the major independent research companies. Historically, proprietary control of metrics has led to distortion and hypoing.

Each country in the world is at a different stage of employment of metrics for measuring media. In Africa there is still significant difficulty with basic infrastructure like electricity, limiting television reach. China has recently established, in conjunction with TNS, traditional TV ratings in the main metropolitan areas. Industrialised countries like the United Kingdom and the United States, however, have mature measurement markets that are now trying to deal with a digital environment.

8 Conclusion

Over 40 years ago, an Advertising Research Foundation (ARF) committee headed by Dr Seymour Banks, director of media research at Leo Burnett in the United States, created a model for evaluating media. That model was divided into six stages:

1. Distribution of the media advertising vehicle;
2. Audience exposure to the vehicle;
3. Audience exposure to a specific advertisement in the vehicle;
4. Audience members' perception of the advertisement;
5. Communication of the advertising message to the audience;
6. Eventual decision regarding whether to purchase the advertised item.

There have been attempts by the ARF to update this model (Phelps, 1989; ARF White Papers, 2009), but exposure is still perceived as the key to making decisions about buying and selling in the media. The new media environment poses challenges to measurement of exposure and what, indeed, will count as currency in new business models. However, despite arguments about 'fractionation' of audiences it is unlikely that the 'mass audience' will disappear in metrics.

Schultz and Kitchen (2000) argue that the marketing and communication manager of the twenty-first century must recognise that there are multiple markets, multiple marketplaces, multiple customers, multiple channels, multiple media. Multiple measurements can doubtless be added to this list. The need for Case Rich audience and customer data, however, remains essential in any assessment of ROI. Integrated brand communications strategists need to be wary about environs where available metrics may be Data Rich but Case Poor.

Facebook, for example, planned to exploit the private information of its 150 million members by creating one of the world's largest market research databases. In an attempt to further fiscally capitalise on the explosion in popularity of the social networking site, once valued at A$24 billion, it would allow multinational companies to selectively target its members in order to research the appeal of new products. Companies would have been able to pose questions to specially selected members based on such intimate details as whether they are single or married and even whether they are gay or straight (Musil, 2009).

In February 2009, Facebook made amendments to its privacy settings that allowed them to take ownership of anything users posted onto their profile – even if they deleted their accounts (Walters, 2009). Users were outraged and protested against the social networking giant. Mark Zuckerberg, the founder, issued a statement saying, 'trust us, we're not doing this to profit from you, it's so we are legally protected as we enable you to share content with other users and services' (Walters, 2009). Needless to say, users were not happy to just 'trust' the CEO of a billion dollar company and Facebook reverted back to its old privacy policies. Zuckerberg subsequently set up a poll asking users to vote on new privacy policies as he still feels they need to be updated (Musil, 2009).

What we see in the Facebook experience is what history has told us about audiences and the media industry. Audiences are sensitive about how they are represented and how information about them is collected and used. The metrics associated with audiences – how they are measured and how the information is captured – are directly related to how decisions are made about advertising, programming and the provision of services. Facebook, in short, came up against what traditional broadcasting has experienced for decades. The difference is, of course, that individuals have a more intimate link to broadcasting of their identities through social media than they ever did in a world of scheduled programming for radio and television which guaranteed a certain anonymity.

Integrated marketing communications and integrated brand marketing are not just about tactical deployment of media in a campaign. It involves a strategic business infrastructure that can provide clients with long-term knowledge about customers and their communication and media needs and that demonstrates accountability for the euro, pound or dollar spend. This includes, of course, an understanding of the strengths and weaknesses of different metrics and their underlying collection rationale.

9 Acknowledgements

Research for this chapter was drawn from the Australian Research Council (ARC) Discovery grant the Emergence, Development and Transformation of Media Ratings Conventions and Methodologies in Australia, 1930–2008.

The author also thanks Professor Peter Miller, Northwestern University, for his insights into his current ratings research, presented as part of the ARC work, at a seminar in Brisbane, Australia, in 2009.

References

Advertising Research Foundation (ARF) (2009). On the Road to a New Effectiveness Model: Measuring Emotional Responses to Television Advertising. Retrieved 16 December.

Arbitron Reaches PPM Settlements In Two States (2009). *Hispanic Market Weekly*, January 12, Retrieved 30 November, http://www.hispanicmarket weekly.com/article.cms?id=10350.

Balnaves, M. (2001). *Introduction to Quantitative Research Methods*. London: Sage.

Balnaves, M. and O'Regan, T. (2009). Comparing Television Ratings Conventions: Australian and American Approaches to Broadcast Ratings. ANZCA09: Communication, Creativity and Global Citizenship. July, Brisbane.

Barbara Caemmerer, B. (2009). 'The Planning and Implementation of Integrated Marketing Communications', *Marketing Intelligence & Planning* 27(4), 524–538.

Beville, H.M. (1985). *Audience Ratings: Radio, Television, Cable*. Hillsdale, N.J.: Lawrence Erlbaum.

Bold, B. (2009). Rate of decline in ad spend slows for consecutive quarters, says Bellwether, *Mediaweek*, mediaweek.co.uk, 13 July, Retrieved 30 November, http://www.mediaweek.co.uk/News/EmailThisArticle/919619/Rate-decline-ad-spend-slows-consecutive-quarters-says-Bellwether

Bodey, M. (2008). 'Ratings System for the Future', *The Australian*, March 20.

Bogart, L. (1966). 'Is It Time to Discard the Audience Concept?' *Journal of Marketing*, 30, January, 47–54.

Businessweek (2006). Web Numbers: What's Real? Competing methods of measuring traffic online leave advertisers, investors, and even Net companies almost flying blind, 23 October, Retrieved 30 November, http://www.businessweek.com/magazine/content/06_43/b4006095.htm.

Clark, N. (2009). Online advertising overtakes TV sales for first time ever. Paid-for search, led by Google, is proving 'recession-friendly'. *The Independent*, 30 September 2009, Retrieved 30 November, http://www.independent.co.uk/news/media/advertising/online-advertising-overtakes-tv-sales-for-first-time-ever-1795274.html.

Crossley, H. (2008). Interviewed by Mark Balnaves. *Tape recording*, 15 October.

Gluck, A. and Pellegrini, P. (2008). Using RFID technology to passively measure print readership: An analysis of Arbitron's lab and field tests. Polls for the public good. *American Association for Public Opinion Research, 63rd Annual Conference*, 15–18 May, New Orleans.

Harris, R. & Seldon, A. (1954). *Advertising in a free society*. London: Institute of Economic Affairs.

Jones, J.P. (1995) 'Single-source Research Begins to Fulfil Its Promise', *Journal of Advertising Research*, 35 (3), 9–16.

Kirby, S.F. (2007). How Traditional Media Can Survive, Monetize and Grow Profits in the Digital Age. Interep NAB.

Miller, P.V. (1994). Made-to-order and standardized audiences: Forms of reality in audience measurement. J.S. Ettema & D.C. Whitney (eds) *Audiencemaking: How the Media Create the Audience* (57–74). London: Sage.

Miller, P.V. (2009). US Electronic Media Audience Ratings: a view from the inside. Ratings Seminar, Centre for Critical and Cultural Studies, July 16, University of Queensland.

Musil, S. (2009, April 16). Facebook opens up vote on new terms of service. Retrieved 21 April 2009 from http://news.cnet.com/8301-1023_3-10221676-93.html.

Napoli, P.M. (2003). *Audience Economics: Media Institutions and the Audience Marketplace*. Columbia: Columbia University Press.

Phelps, S. (1989). 'A Reconsideration of the ARF Model', *Marketing & Media Decisions*, November 98.

Schultz, D.E. and Kitchen, P.J. (2000). *Communicating Globally: An Integrated Marketing Approach*, Basingstoke: Macmillan.

Story, L. (2008). Nielsen looks beyond TV, and hits roadblocks. *New York Times*, 26 February.

Walters, C. (2009, February 15). Facebook's new terms of service: 'We can do anything we want with your content. Forever'. Message posted to www.consumerist.com. Industry blog. Retrieved 21 April 2009.

Webster, J.G., Phalen, P.F. & Lichty, L.W. (2000). *Ratings Analysis: The Theory and Practice of Audience Research*. Hillsdale, N.J.: Lawrence Erblaum.

Vollmer and Rothenberg (2007). *The Future of Advertising*. Booz Allen Hamilton.

Index

Note: Locators in *italics* refers to diagrams and tables cited in the text. 'n' followed by locators refers to notes in the text.